TABLE OF CONTENTS

INTRODUCTION   7
1. AMAZON RIVER   8
    Brazil/Peru

2. THE ANDES   9
    South America

3. ANGEL FALLS (CHURUN MERU)   10
    Venezuela

4. ANKARANA PLATEAU   11
    Madagascar

5. ANTARCTICA   12
    Antarctica

6. ARCHES NATIONAL PARK   13
    Utah, USA

7. ATACAMA DESERT   14
    Chile

8. Earth'S ATMOSPHERE   15

9. AURORA BOREALIS and
    AURORA AUSTRALIS   16
    The Earth's Poles

10. AYERS ROCK (ULURU)   17
    Australia

11. LAKE BAIKAL   18
    Russia

12. LAKE BALATON   19
    Hungary

13. BOUVET ISLAND   20
    South Atlantic

14. CARLSBAD CAVERNS   21
    New Mexico, USA

15. CASPIAN SEA   22
    Central Asia

16. CHALLENGER DEEP   23
    Pacific Ocean

17. CHIMBORAZO   24
    Ecuador

18. CRATER LAKE   25
    Oregon, USA

19. CROCKER LAND   26
    The Arctic

20. DEAD SEA   27
    Jordan/Israel

21. DEATH VALLEY   28
    California, USA

22. DEVIL'S TOWER   29
    Wyoming, USA

23. DZUNGARIA   30
    Xinjiang Uygur, China

24. MOUNT EVEREST
    (SAGARMATHA, QOMOLANGMA)   31
    Nepal/Tibet

25. THE EVERGLADES *32*
Florida, USA

26. MOUNT FUJI *33*
Japan

27. BAY OF FUNDY *34*
Canada

28. GANGES (GANGA or GANGAJI)
RIVER *35*
India

29. GIANT'S CAUSEWAY *36*
Northern Ireland

30. THE GRAND CANYON *37*
Arizona, USA

31. GREAT BARRIER REEF *38*
Australia

32. THE GREAT FUNGUS *39*
Michigan, USA

33. THE GREAT LAKES *40*
USA/Canada

34. GREAT SALT LAKE *41*
Utah, USA

35. GREENLAND ICE SHEET *42*
Greenland

36. LAKE HILLIER *43*
Australia

37. HUANG HO (YELLOW) RIVER *44*
China

38. ICE ISLAND T.1 and the
ICE ISLAND OF 1956 *45*
South Pacific

39. IGUAZU FALLS *46*
Brazil/Argentina

40. INDUS RIVER *47*
Pakistan

41. KALAHARI DESERT *48*
Botswana

42. KILAUEA VOLCANO *49*
Hawaii, USA

43. MOUNT KILIMANJARO *50*
Tanzania/Kenya

44. KINGS CANYON *51*
California, USA

45. KLONDIKE RIVER *52*
Yukon Territory, Canada

46. KRAKATOA (KRAKATAU) *53*
Indonesia

47. LA BREA TAR PITS *54*
California, USA

48. LAKE LADOGA *55*
Russia

49. LASSEN PEAK *56*
California, USA

50. LONG VALLEY CALDERA *57*
California, USA

51. MAMMOTH CAVE *58*
Kentucky, USA

52. THE MATTERHORN
(MONTE CERVINO) *59*
Switzerland

53. MAUNA KEA *60*
Hawaii, USA

54. MAUNA LOA *61*
Hawaii, USA

55. MOUNT McKINLEY (DENALI) *62*
Alaska, USA

56. MEGHALAYA *63*
India

57. MISSISSIPPI RIVER *64*
United States

58. MISSOURI RIVER *65*
United States

59. CLIFFS OF MOHER *66*
Ireland

60. MONO LAKE *67*
California, USA

61. THE MOTHER LODE *68*
California, USA

62. NAMIB DESERT *69*
Namibia

63. NIAGARA FALLS *70*
Canada / USA

64. NILE RIVER *71*
Africa

65. NOHOCH NA CHICH *72*
Mexico

66. NOVARUPTA *73*
Alaska, USA

67. OKAVANGO DELTA *74*
Botswana

68. THE PACIFIC OCEAN *75*

69. THE PRIPET MARSHES *76*
Russia/Belarus

70. PULAU BATU HAIRAN *77*
Malaysia

71. MOUNT RAINIER *78*
Washington, USA

72. MOUNT REDOUBT *79*
Alaska, USA

73. RED SPRITES and BLUE JETS *80*
High in the atmosphere

74. RHINE (RHEIN) RIVER *81*
Europe

75. THE RING OF FIRE *82*
Pacific Basin

76. RITTEN (RENON) *83*
Austria/Italy/France

77. SAHARA DESERT *84*
Africa

78. MOUNT ST. HELENS   *85*
    Washington, USA

79. SAN ANDREAS FAULT   *86*
    California, USA

80. SANTORINI   *87*
    Aegean Sea

81. SARAWAK CHAMBER   *88*
    Malaysia

82. SARGASSO SEA   *89*
    Atlantic Ocean

83. THE SEQUOIAS   *90*
    California, USA

84. LAKE SUPERIOR   *91*
    USA/Canada

85. THE TEPUIS   *92*
.   Venezuela

86. TIGRIS-EUPHRATES VALLEY   *93*
    Iraq

87. LAKE TITICACA   *94*
    Peru

88. TONGA TRENCH SEAMOUNT   *95*
    South Pacific

89. TRIPLE DIVIDE   *96*
    Montana, USA

90. TRISTAN DA CUNHA   *97*
    South Atlantic

91. MOUNT VESUVIUS   *98*
    Italy

92. VICTORIA (MOSIOATUNYA) FALLS   *99*
    Zambia

93. WAIMANGU (BLACK WATER)
    GEYSER   *100*
    New Zealand

94. WEDDELL SEA   *101*
    Antarctica

95. WEST WIND DRIFT CURRENT   *102*
    Antarctica/South Atlantic

96. YANGTZE RIVER (CHANG JIANG)   *103*
    China

97. YELLOW MOUNTAIN
    (HUANG SHAN)   *104*
    China

98. YELLOWSTONE   *105*
    Wyoming, USA

99. YOSEMITE VALLEY   *106*
    California, USA

100. ZAÏRE RIVER   *107*
    Zaïre

INTRODUCTION

The natural world is a wonderful place, filled with amazing features and spectacular sights. The majesty of snow-capped mountains and vast canyons contrasts with the terror of Volcanos and the mystery of subterranean caves or chambers. The natural world is a wonderland of contrasts. There are the great rivers of the world, such as the Nile, which brought life to the world's largest desert, the Rhine that gave a national identity to a nation that contains neither its source nor its mouth, and the Zaïre River, which has frightened travellers for centurics.

There are the places in our world that defy belief, such as the plateau in Madagascar that has never been explored because anyone who tried would be cut to shreds, or the underground room in Malaysia where the Houston Astrodome would seem small.

There are features so large that they cannot be seen in their entirety from any vantage point on Earth, such as the Pacific Ocean, a body of water that accounts for a third of our planet's surface area or the atmosphere itself, which surrounds the entire planet and makes life possible. These contrast with Crocker Land in the Arctic whose visual impression is very misleading and the Tonga Seamount, the tallest mountain on Earth that no one has ever seen.

There is a place on Earth can you find a naturally-occurring group of spindly stone pillars a yard wide at the base and taller than the surrounding trees — and each one has a boulder twice its own diameter balanced on its peak. There are monoliths, or gargantuan "single rocks," around whom legends of the supernatural have been associated. There are places in Ireland and the United States where there are naturally-occurring six-sided solid stone columns that appear to have been hewn by human hands.

There is a place in the heart of a major American city where the bodies of long-extinct saber-toothed tigers from the Pleistocene epoch lie preserved in asphalt. This contrasts to the place that Mark Twain called the "loneliest place on Earth," where slabs of volcanic rock float in thick, salty water and the islands are covered with steaming vents of hot springs and with frozen white forests of calcium carbonate.

This book is a celebration of the wonder of our natural world, as seen from the vantage points of the most spectacular, the most remarkable and the most thought-provoking environments on our Earth.

A striking view of Earth, taken from the Apollo 8 spacecraft.

AMAZON RIVER
Brazil/Peru

In terms of volume, the **Amazon** (or in Spanish or Portuguese, **Amazonas**) is the largest river in the world. With origins in the Andes of Peru and in countless tributaries throughout Brazil, it flows 4,000 miles (6,440 kilometers) to the Atlantic Ocean, although the entire Amazon system of tributaries probably have a total length of 50,000 miles (80,500 kilometers), roughly half of which is navigable.

The Amazon drains into the Atlantic, but has its source within 100 miles (160 kilometers) of the Pacific. It is the dominant geographical feature in northern South America, and has a drainage area that encompasses 2.5 million square miles (6.5 million square kilometers).

The **Marañón River**, which is generally regarded as the upper course of the Amazon, originates in the Andes northeast of Lima at an altitude of 14,000 feet (4,300 meters). It is navigable only 200 miles (320 kilometers) from the Pacific and by large boats east of Iquitos. From the Brazilian border to the city of Manaus, the Amazon is known as the **Solimoes**.

Major tributaries include the **Yavari, Jutahy, Jurua, Purus** and the **Madeira** (largest of the tributaries) to the south, and the **Ica (Putumayo), Japura** and **Negro** to the north. At its mouth, the great Amazon intersects the **Tocantins**, an inland waterway that runs 1,500 miles from north to south.

Having tumbled in waterfalls from the high Andes, the Amazon's last 2,000 miles (3,200 kilometers) is generally flat and placid, with few rapids. It flows from three to five mph (five to eight kph) except in floods. The Amazon is often so wide and calm that it appears like a *lake*. Upstream from Manaus, the Amazon may be two to four miles (three to six kilometers) across, but it widens to 15 miles while still well upstream from the Atlantic, and is 50 miles (80 kilometers) wide at its mouth.

Most of the vast Amazon region is characterized as being tropical or subtropical in nature, and it includes the great **Amazon Rain Forest**, the largest rain forest in the world. The Amazon was first explored by Europeans during the 1540 expedition of **Francisco de Orellana,** who named it for the Amazons, women warriors of Greek mythology, after he saw armed native women on the shore. Today the region is subject to often-controversial mining and lumbering activities.

The great Amazon Rain Forest is filled with wildlife, including the Anaconda snake.

The highest mountain range on Earth is the **Himalaya/Karakoram Range**, which is located in Tibet and Bhutan and touches parts of Nepal, India and China. The tallest mountain in the world — **Mount Everest** (see no. 24) — is here. So indeed are the 35 tallest mountains in the world, and the top 62, if you count ranges that are considered spurs of the Himalaya/Karakoram Range.

However, these 62 peaks are located on a vast plateau, nearly the size of continental Europe, where the valley floors have an average elevation of 16,000 feet (5,000 meters). If you deduct this plateau elevation from the lofty heights of the individual Himalaya/Karakoram peaks, then another range emerges as an amazing wonder, this one with more than 35 peaks that are taller than those in Asia.

While the Himalaya/Karakoram Range is located deep in the heart of the Asian land mass, the **Andes** of South America rise only 50 to 100 miles (80 to 160 kilometers) above the **Pacific Ocean's** sea level.

The Andes contain an amazing total of 29 mountains, which, outside of Asia's great plateau, are taller than any mountain on Earth. These include the mighty **Aconcagua**, the tallest mountain in South America at 22,834 feet (6,960 meters), and **Mount Chimborazo** (see no. 17), whose peak is farther from the Earth's center than any other place on our planet.

The Andes are also the longest mountain range on Earth, stretching for over 4,500 miles (7,200 kilometers) and containing many active and dormant volcanos. The average height of the range exceeds 12,000 feet (3,700 meters), and the world's highest navigable lake, **Titicaca** (see no. 87), is located in the Andes. (See map on page 14.)

The Andes Mountains in Argentina.

3. ANGEL FALLS
Venezuela

Twice as high as **Yosemite Falls** and 30 times as high as **Niagara Falls**, this incredible Venezuelan waterfall is the world's highest, falling nearly a *mile*, or roughly 5,000 feet (1,500 meters), with 3,212 feet (979 meters) being a straight, uninterrupted fall.

Angel Falls was known to natives for centuries as **Churun Meru**, but first reported to the outside world in November 1933 by the American pilot and adventurer **Jimmy Angel**, for whom it is named. The falls are fed by water flowing off the 300 square miles (780 square kilometers) **Auyan Tepui** plateau in the **Guinea Highlands**, and flow into the **Churun (Caroni) River**. The plateau is extremely wet, with rainfall of about 300 inches (762 centimeters) annually.

The remoteness of the falls is demonstrated by the story of Angel's second flight to the falls. He and his wife along with two Venezuelan mountaineers flew to the region and established a base camp with a radio. Leaving one of the mountaineers, they flew to the falls, attempted to land above it, got stuck in a bog and had to walk out. It took two weeks just to reach the base camp!

It was not until 1949, however, that an expedition to the region led by war correspondent **Ruth Robertson** measured Angel Falls and officially confirmed it as the world's tallest.

Angel Falls.

There are some places on Earth where the natural features are so strange that they cannot be believed. Strange is defined here as being so unusual that it is considered impossible and therefore fictitious. However, truth is stranger than fiction, and this fact is proven at the northern tip of the island of Madagascar off the coast of Africa in a place called **Tsingy** on the **Ankarana Plateau**.

Madagascar itself is a strange place from the point of view of its natural history. Like Australia, it was cut off from the mainland. Living species evolved here that are similar to, but unlike those of Africa, 375 miles (600 kilometers) away. Here are the world's only **crocodiles** that live in caves, and the **tenrecs**, tiny creatures that look like hedgehogs and have spines like raccoons. And there are several species of **lemurs**, engaging little creatures that are described as being like both cats and monkeys, and which are actually primates, related to apes and humans.

On the Ankarana Plateau, there is a vast region that is home to lemurs, but which has never been explored on foot by humans. Indeed it never will be, as there is literally no level place to step. On this plateau, there is an area larger than the state of Rhode Island where the landscape consists of only narrow limestone spikes, some of them as high as 100 feet (30 meters), and nearly all taller than a person.

Known as the Tsingy region because of the clanging sound made when one of the spikes is tapped with a metal tool, the area is an impenetrable maze. There is no place to step between the spikes, which are as sharp as steak knives, and if one did manage to penetrate the labyrinth without being cut to shreds, the probability of becoming hopelessly lost or bitten by poisonous snakes makes death a near certainty.

The unusual tenrec of Madagascar.

11

5. ANTARCTICA
Antarctica

It is the world's fifth largest continent (5.4 million square miles/14.1 million square kilometers), and a land mass half again larger than Europe. **Antarctica** is also the strangest of all continents. Indeed, it is so unlike any other place on Earth that it is like another planet. The well-publicized hole in the ozone layer above Antarctica makes it a place more like the planet Mars than the planet Earth, a place where solar ultraviolet radiation can reach the surface virtually unimpeded.

Antarctica is unique in many other ways. While whales are seen in the waters offshore, it is the only continent without any indigenous land mammals. Also, unlike all other continents, it has never had an indigenous human population, and few people have ever set foot there. In fact, all of the people who have ever visited Antarctica would fit comfortably in the seats of a large sports stadium. The number who have lived there through the summer (the coldest period) could fit easily in a large room.

The most important geographical fact about Antarctica is that it contains the Earth's **South Geographic Pole** and **South Magnetic Pole**. Because Antarctica also has the worst weather on Earth, it was not until 1911 that a team led by Norwegian explorer **Roald Amundsen** became the first humans to reach the South Pole. The first person to lead an expedition that set foot on the continent was the Russian admiral **Fabian Gottlieb von Bellingshausen**, who arrived in 1821, but it was not until the winter (the warmest time in the Southern Hemisphere) of 1957-1958 that the New Zealand explorer **Sir Edmund Hillary** led a team across the continent by land.

Antarctica is by far the coldest continent on Earth, with an average temperature below zero on both the Fahrenheit and Centigrade scales. The coldest temperature ever recorded on Earth was at **Vostok Station**, 750 miles (1,200 kilometers) inland, on July 21, 1983, when the mercury dropped to -128.6 degrees F (-89.2 degrees C). **Plateau Station** in Antarctica has the world's coldest annual average temperatures: -70 degrees F (-57 degrees C). The warmest temperature ever recorded was 59 degrees F (15 degrees C) at **Vanda Station** on January 5, 1974.

Antarctica's most outstanding feature is, of course, the **Antarctic Ice Sheet**, the world's biggest single slab of ice, which covers an area equal to the size of the entire continent of Europe to a depth of up to two miles (three kilometers). It is also the driest continent on Earth, with only an inch (2.5 centimeters) of annual precipitation. Over billions of years, this scant snowfall has gradually created the Ice Sheet.

With the Ice Sheet in mind, one of the most unique areas on this unique continent are the dry valleys of **Victoria Land,** where there is no ice nor accumulated snow. There are, however, salty, ice-covered lakes in these rugged, rocky valleys, where the ice produced a greenhouse effect that warms the water beneath to temperatures well above that of the air above the ice.

6. ARCHES NATIONAL PARK
Utah, USA

With the greatest density of naturally occurring stone arches in the world, this spectacular site is both visually exciting and geologically intriguing. Over the course of 100 million years, the erosive forces of wind and water have created a wonderland of over 1500 red sandstone arches.

The arches range in size from several with openings of about three feet (one meter) to the awesome **Landscape Arch**, which arcs 306 feet (93 meters) from end to end. Among the largest and most spectacular is **Delicate Arch**. One of the thinnest and most fragile of the big arches, it became even more so in 1991, when a 60-foot (18-meter) slab of stone fell from the underside of the arch. Eventually the center will crumble, and Delicate Arch will be gone forever.

This vast concentration originated with a salt bed deposited 3,000 million years ago when Utah was covered by an inland sea. The water evaporated, leaving the salt, which was in turn covered by layers of silt, which became sandstone. The weight of the sandstone caused the salt, as well as the sandstone atop it, to shift and buckle.

Water running in the long cracks that occurred in the sandstone gradually created long, thin sandstone walls, or **fins**. Over time, water running in the channels between the fins eroded holes at the base of the fins. The holes became larger and larger, creating the spectacular arches. Eventually the arches become so thin that they collapse, as many have already done, and as Delicate Arch will in the future.

This 66,344-acre (26,849-hectare) site north of Moab, Utah was designated at a US National Monument in 1929, and became a US National Park in 1971. Other important sites are **Natural Bridges** and **Rainbow Bridge**, also in Utah. The latter spans 275 feet (84 meters) and arches to a height of 290 feet (88 meters). These sites were respectively designated as US National Monuments in 1908 and 1910.

Delicate Arch, Arches National Park, Utah.

ATACAMA DESERT
Chile

Lying in a vast and parched basin between the **Andes** and the coastal ranges, the **Atacama Desert** is a dry and foreboding place. In fact, it is the driest place on earth!

Indeed, no rainfall was recorded here for the *401 years* between 1570 and 1971, and there are some places where no rain has ever been recorded.

The Atacama, at an elevation of 2000 feet (610 meters), spreads across the Chilean provinces of Antofagasta, Atacama and Tarapaca. Its economic importance is derived solely from mining, and the mineral wealth ranges from nitrates and borax to ores containing such metals as copper, silver, iron, lead and nickel.

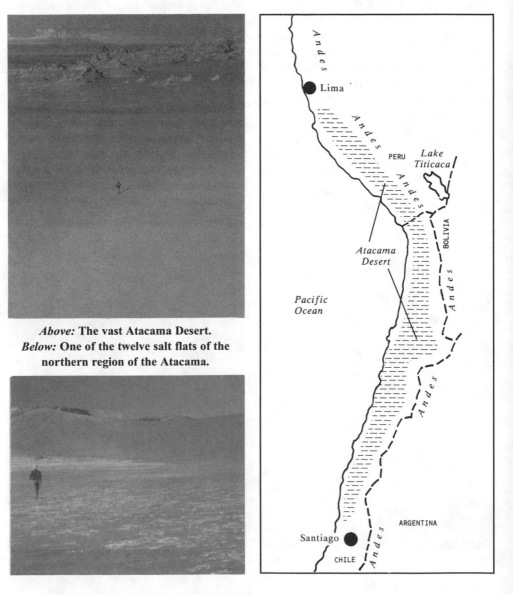

Above: **The vast Atacama Desert.**
Below: **One of the twelve salt flats of the northern region of the Atacama.**

8. AURORA BOREALIS & AURORA AUSTRALIS The Earth's Poles

On a dark night in the far northern or southern latitudes, one may see strange and mysterious shimmering colored lights in the sky. Unlike the lights of a near-distant city reflecting off haze or clouds, these lights flicker and move as though someone is moving a giant searchlight just beyond the horizon. Also unlike the lights of a near-distant city reflecting off haze or clouds, these lights usually appear over uninhabited areas.

They are decidedly strange, ranging from the barely-visible-in-the-distance to lights that fill the entire sky and seem to come so close that you can touch them. They vary in color. They are often white, but frequently they have a greenish, purplish or yellowish tint. What are they?

They were named **Aurora**, after the Roman goddess of the dawn. In the North, they are **Aurora Borealis**, or **Northern Lights**, while in the Southern Hemisphere, they are the **Aurora Australis**, or the **Southern Lights**.

What causes them was long a subject of conjecture. Once they were attributed to gods or sorcerers, and later it was suggested that they were caused by sunlight reflecting off the polar ice caps. In fact they are caused by charged particles released from the **sun** during periods of intense **sunspot** activity. These collide with oxygen and hydrogen atoms in the Earth's atmosphere at altitudes ranging from 50 to 80 miles (80 to 130 kilometers), and occasionally as high as 190 miles (310 kilometers) where the atmosphere is virtually non-existent.

The Aurora Australis as photographed from the Space Shuttle Discovery's flightdeck.

15

9. EARTH'S ATMOSPHERE

Among the **Solar System's** solid-surfaced planets and major moons, there are mountains and canyons that rival the greatest that the Earth has to offer. On **Mars**, a canyon called the **Valles Marinaris (Mariner Valley)** looks like our **Grand Canyon**, but is long enough to stretch across the United States. Also on Mars is **Olympus Mons (Mount Olympus)**, a dormant volcano that is similar to **Mauna Kea**, but is taller than Mauna Kea and **Mount Everest** combined. Several of the moons on **Jupiter** and **Saturn** have ice sheets larger than **Antarctica**, and **Jupiter's** moon **Io** is so volcanically active that eruptions are almost continuous.

There are even several bodies in the Solar System that have atmospheres. The four biggest planets, the "gas giants," are *all* atmosphere, but among solid-surfaced bodies, Mars and **Triton** have atmospheres less dense than ours, while those on **Venus** and **Titan** are denser.

What only the Earth has is an atmosphere with a unique combination of gasses that sustain life. It is thought that Mars may have had this and Titan may evolve to this, but we have it now and will continue to have it for a very long time.

What is our atmosphere? It is a gaseous layer composed of 78 percent nitrogen and 21 percent oxygen, with the balance being mostly carbon dioxide, argon and water vapor. It is estimated to weigh 5,700 trillion tons (5,800 trillion metric tons). Half of

the atmosphere's weight is found below the elevation of 18,000 feet (5,500 meters), while 99 percent is located below 100,000 feet (30,000 meters). The atmosphere is generally held to be 633,000 feet (193,000 meters) thick — the altitude above which orbital spacecraft operate — although traces of atmospheric gasses exist beyond this for about 400 miles (640 kilometers).

The layers within the atmosphere, starting from the earth's surface, are the **troposphere** (up to seven miles/11 kilometers), the **stratosphere** (seven-30 miles/11-48 kilometers), the **mesosphere** (30-50 miles/48-80 kilometers) and the **thermosphere** (50-400 miles/80-645 kilometers). Beyond these is the region of interplanetary space known as the **exosphere**. Most species exist in the troposphere, and nothing on earth can survive above the stratosphere's lower levels, as the atmospheric thinness does not contain enough concentrated oxygen. Among humans, survival in the stratosphere is possible through the use of bottled oxygen (see no. 24).

Cloud formations in the Earth's atmosphere.

AYERS ROCK (ULURU)
Australia

The middle of the continent of Australia is characterized by the vast **Australian Desert** which spreads across 600,000 square miles (1,550,000 square kilometers) and is almost entirely flat. Imagine the surprise then of someone crossing this enormous flatness and coming upon a gigantic boulder lying at almost the exact geographical center of the continent.

Known and revered for centuries to the aboriginal people as **Uluru**, this great monolith was first glimpsed by Europeans in the 1870s. These men, Ernest Giles and William Gosse, named it **Ayers Rock** after South Australia's prime minister, Sir Henry Ayers, although the rock actually lies in the Northern Territory near the town of Alice Springs.

Though it looks like a boulder and is often reported as such, Ayers Rock is not a rock, but rather an outcropping of subterranean sandstone, which has yet to be eroded into sand and gravel like the surrounding desert. It is like the blunted tip of a huge stone iceberg, as there is much more of it beneath the surface.

Ayers rock rises 1,142 feet (348 meters) above the surrounding desert and is two miles (three kilometers) across and six miles (10 kilometers) around.

An important national landmark, Ayers Rock is also an extremely sacred site for the Aboriginal people, a fact which has come into conflict with increasing tourism.

Ayers Rock as viewed across the Australian Desert.

LAKE BAIKAL
Russia

The world's deepest lake is also the largest freshwater lake on the Eurasian land mass. An ancient lake dating from perhaps as early as the Jurassic Period, **Lake Baikal** encompasses an area of 12,162 square miles (31,499 square kilometers). It measures 395 miles (635 kilometers) long, 49 miles (79 kilometers) wide at its widest point, and as deep as 6,365 feet (1,940 meters) below sea level. The waters are especially clear, making it possible to see to a depth of 130 feet (40 meters).

The major rivers feeding Lake Baikal are the **Upper Angara, Barguzin** and **Selenga**, but the only outflow is through the mighty **Tunguska** (**Angara**). The lake is largely surrounded by steep, mountainous terrain, except for the area around the Selenga's mouth.

There is considerable ship traffic on the lake in summer, but it remains mostly frozen from December to May, when there is surface traffic across the ice.

Lake Baikal provides a rich fishing ground, and the lake is large enough to support its own species of seal, which is related to the Caspian and Arctic species.

Economically, the lake is centered on one of Siberia's most developed mining and lumbering areas, with the southern edge of the lake being served by the Transsiberian Railway.

Lake Baikal abounds in marine life: Seals, salmon, herring and the massive sturgeon.

LAKE BALATON
Hungary

The largest lake in central Europe is known informally as "the Hungarian Ocean" because of both its size and the peculiar microclimate surrounding it. The latter includes sudden, violent storms during most of the year that stir up huge, ocean-like waves, although in winter the lake usually freezes.

Lake Balaton encompasses an area of 230 square miles (600 square kilometers), measuring 48 miles (77 kilometers) long and eight miles (13 kilometers) wide at its widest point. This strange European "ocean" is fed by the **Sala River**. Lake Balaton's outflow goes into the great **Danube River** via the **Sio River**.

The earliest known major settlements on its shore were built by the prehistoric Avar people, although others, including the Romans and Magyars, have built towns and forts here. The lake is now a resort and fishing area. Fishing includes the **fogas**, which are considered a local delicacy.

A view from the shoreline of beautiful Lake Balaton.

There is a phrase in the vernacular about getting "away from it all" that describes "going to a desert island." In fact, most of the world's islands are reasonably close to either major land masses or other islands. While modern transportation and communications have ensured that most islands are no longer "islands," island life remains detached, although not as detached as it once was.

In terms of island remoteness, however, **Bouvet Island** is an island apart. From here, the nearest land is Antarctica's Queen Maud Land, which is uninhabited and 1,050 miles (1,700 kilometers) away. Bouvet Island is over 2,500 miles (4,000 kilometers) away from Africa.

A Norwegian dependency, Bouvet Island is a slab of volcanic rock in the South Atlantic that was discovered on January 1, 1739 by **J.B.C. Bouvet de Lozier**, who did not set foot upon its ugly shore. The first to do so was **Captain George Norris**, who landed here on December 16, 1825 and left soon after. Today no one lives on Bouvet Island and it receives few visitors. The most remote *inhabited* island is **Tristan da Cunha** (see no. 90), which is also in the South Atlantic.

Seagulls nest on nearly every rock of the world's oceans, however remote.

Located beneath the Guadalupe Mountains, this natural underground labyrinth is several miles long and the largest of its kind yet to be discovered in the world. It has 76 separate, known caves and many peripheral regions that are still unexplored. **Carlsbad Caverns** exist on three levels, averaging 750, 900 and 1,320 feet (230, 270 and 400 meters) beneath the surface. Its deepest point is 1,565 feet (480 meters) below the surface.

The largest single room is the appropriately-named **Big Room**, a cross-shaped grotto 1,800 feet by 1,100 feet (550 by 340 meters), with the ceiling's peak rising 255 feet (80 meters) above the floor.

The story of Carlsbad goes back 250 million years, to the time of a 400-mile (640-kilometer) reef in an inland sea. Buried under layers of salt and gypsum, as the sea evaporated, the buried reef's limestone residue was gradually eroded by the salty, corrosive water.

Over the past 500,000 years, after the caverns themselves were carved out of the rock, thousands of pillars, stalactites and stalagmites were formed, drop by drop of minute quantities of minerals dissolved in water. The largest of these are **Giant Dome**, a 62-foot (19-meter) stalag-

Above: **New Cave.**
Below: **The Bifrost Room.**

mite, and the 42-foot (13-meter) **Twin Domes**. The caverns are also home to 300,000 **Mexican Free-tail Bats**, whose nightly exodus from the caverns' natural opening is a major tourist attraction.

The caverns, known to the ancient native people of the region, were rediscovered by settlers in the nineteenth century. The first extensive exploration of the Carlsbad Caverns was undertaken by **Jim White** around 1910, but major, previously-unexplored rooms were discovered in 1966, 1982 and 1984. Carlsbad Caverns became a U.S. National Monument in 1923 and were redesignated as a national park in 1930. Jim White was Carlsbad's first chief ranger.

CASPIAN SEA
Central Asia

The world's largest inland sea or lake currently has an area of 143,000 square miles (371,000 square kilometers). However, its size steadily decreases due to evaporation and its water being diverted upstream for irrigation. In 1950, its area was 169,000 square miles (438,000 square kilometers)!

Today, the **Caspian Sea** measures 750 miles (1,200 kilometers) long and up to 300 miles (480 kilometers) wide at its widest. At its deepest, the Caspian is over 3,000 feet (900 meters) deep. With the possible exception of the **Himalayas**, it is the most profound defining feature on the Asian continent. At one time, it was connected to the **Aral Sea**, another land-locked salt sea, which is located about 600 miles (960 kilometers) to the east.

The major source feeding the Caspian is the great **Volga River**, but others include the **Ural, Aras** and **Kura Rivers.** The area around the sea is generally mountainous, except for the delta at the Volga's mouth.

The saltiest part of the Caspian is the **Kara-Bogaz-Gol**, a gulf connected to the Caspian's main body by a narrow channel, through which a strong current flows.

Both Alexander the Great and Marco Polo visited the Caspian Sea, and major trade routes have followed its shore. Today it is surrounded by the former Soviet republics of Russia, Kazakhstan, Azerbaijan and Turkmenstan, with Iran to its south. The largest port city on the Caspian is Baku, the capital of Azerbaijan.

Fishing has always been important to the economic life of the people of the Caspian. The caviar of the **Caspian sturgeon** is the most highly prized caviar on Earth. Another important aquatic animal is the **Caspian seal**, a species related to the Baikal and Arctic seals.

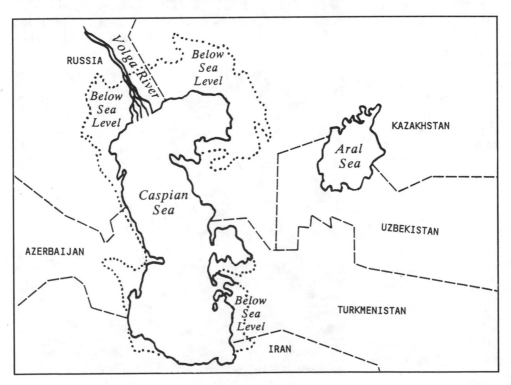

CHALLENGER DEEP
Pacific Ocean

The deepest point on the floor of any of the world's oceans is the **Challenger Deep**, identified by and named for the British oceanographic research ship *Challenger* in 1951. Located in the **Marinas Trench** in the western Pacific Ocean 170 nautical miles (320 kilometers) south of Guam, the Deep was first estimated to be 35,813 feet (10,915 meters) below sea level at its deepest part. This calculation was confirmed in 1984 by the Japanese survey ship *Takuyo*, which used a narrow multi-beam echo sounder to calculate a depth of 35,839 feet (10,923 meters), with a margin of error at plus or minus 33 feet (ten meters).

The first submersible vessel to explore the Deep was the American bathyscaphe *Trieste*, which descended to the bottom in January 1960. As no sunlight penetrates these depths, the species of fish discovered here are completely sightless.

The Deep's water pressure would make a 2.2 pound (one kilogram) steel ball fall for over an hour before reaching the Deep's bottom from the ocean's surface!

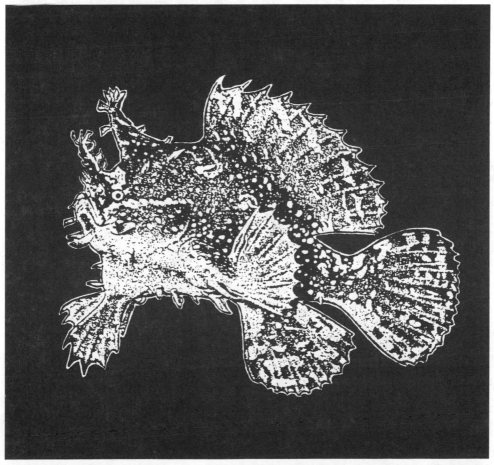

An early concept of one of the strange fish residing in the deepest parts of the Pacific Ocean.

CHIMBORAZO
Ecuador

To tell this story is to dash widely-believed notions about the Earth's physical nature. Most people know that the two tallest mountains on Earth are the Himalayan **Mount Everest** and **K2**, whose summits are respectively recorded in the *Guinness Book of Records* as measuring 29,078 feet (8,862 meters) and 28,238 feet (8,607 meters) above sea level.

It would logically follow that these two summits would be the two most distant spots from the Earth's center. Wrong. These two summits are closer to the Earth's center than the summit of an obscure peak in Ecuador's **Andes Mountains**.

Although one might assume that the Earth is a nearly-perfect sphere, it is not. The Earth's own rotation causes it to bulge outward at the equator. Therefore, a mountain called **Chimborazo**, located just 98 miles

Chimborazo, circa 1920.

(158 kilometers) south of the equator, has a summit 7,057 feet (2,151 meters) farther from the center of the Earth than Mount Everest, even though the Chimborazo is only 20,561 feet (6,267 meters) above sea level.

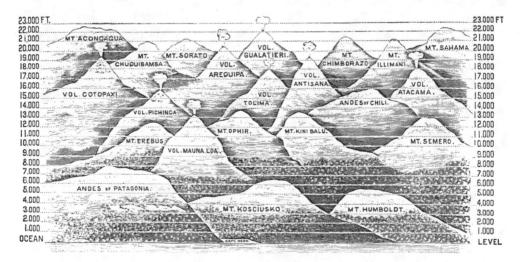

18. CRATER LAKE
Oregon, USA

In 5700 BC, as the first civilizations were developing in Mesopotamia, the snow-capped **Mount Mazama**, one of the Western Hemisphere's highest mountains, literally exploded. Mazama, estimated to have stood over 12,000 feet (3,700 meters) high, was one of the tallest volcanos (along with **Rainier** and **Shasta**) in the **Cascade Range**, the continental U.S.'s most volcanically active region.

Probably the most cataclysmic event ever witnessed by North Americans, the explosion may have been seen and heard throughout much of the continent. It also probably resulted in the deaths of many natives who lived nearby. Over 5,000 square miles (13,000 square kilometers) were covered with volcanic ash at least six inches (15 centimeters) deep. One-third of Mazama's height had turned to dust.

Mazama was gone, replaced by a crater six miles (ten kilometers) across and 3,900 feet (1,200 meters) deep. The highest point on the rim of the crater, now known as **Hillman Peak**, is 8,151 feet (2,484 meters) above sea level.

Volcanic activity continued at the site until about 2000 BC, and then gradually subsided. As it cooled, the crater slowly filled with water, forming what is now **Crater Lake**. **Wizard Island**, on the lake's west side, is a volcanic cone ("a volcano within a volcano") that is still potentially active.

The lake itself is a closed ecosystem. No streams flow into or out of it.

For centuries, Native American shamans kept the lake secret as a sacred site. Few people knew of it until it was accidentally discovered by prospectors in 1853. The lake is now the centerpiece of Crater Lake National Park, established in 1902.

Crater Lake National Park.

In addition to having many strange and wonderful qualities, the world of nature has many amazing places that defy belief. Certainly this was true of **Yellowstone** (see no. 98), an place so unusual that it was long considered to be fictitious. What then of places that appear quite normal, but in fact do not exist at all?

Perhaps the strangest place on Earth is **Crocker Land**, a land mass discovered by polar explorer **Admiral Robert Edwin Peary** on one of his Arctic voyages. He sighted it west of Canada's **Ellesmere Island**, over 1,000 miles (1,600 kilometers) north of the **Arctic Circle**.

Crocker Land was observed again in 1913 by **Donald B. MacMillan**, who described it as a striking mass of "hills, valleys and snow-capped peaks extending through at least 120 degrees of the horizon." In other words, Crocker Land was hundreds of miles or kilometers across, or at least a third of the horizon. While it is not unusual to see snowy mountains in the Arctic, Crocker Land is peculiar, because it *does not exist!*

Crocker Land is a mirage, the largest mirage ever seen. We all are familiar with the phenomenon known as the mirage, an optical illusion caused by the refraction of light through layers of surface air with different temperatures, but seldom is one large enough or distinct enough to be mistaken for reality for more than a moment. To fool someone as experienced as Peary, Crocker Land is amazing indeed.

A mirage of sailing ships and distant lands among the ice floes above the Arctic Circle.

20. DEAD SEA
Jordan/Israel

Five times as salty as the world's oceans, the **Dead Sea** was named based on the belief that its saltiness prevented any aquatic life. This is largely true, although microorganisms have since been detected here.

The shores of the world's saltiest body of water also mark the lowest point on the Earth's land surface, 1,302 feet (397 meters) below sea level. The Dead Sea measures 49 miles (79 kilometers) in length and is up to ten miles (16 kilometers) wide at its widest. It is 1,300 feet (400 meters) deep in the north, but very shallow in the south.

Located in the **Great Rift Valley**, the Dead Sea is fed by the waters of the **Jordan River** and other streams. There is no outflow, only evaporation, which accounts for the saltiness.

The water is so full of salt and other materials that it is virtually impossible for a swimmer to sink. The Romans, believing that the Dead Sea's waters had restorative powers, came here to swim and even drink!

The Dead Sea and Israel as seen from Mount Nebo, photographed by G. Eric Matson, circa 1910.

The lowest point in the Western Hemisphere, **Death Valley** is 282 feet (86 meters) below sea level. Ironically, it is within sight of California's **Mount Whitney**, which is, at 14,494 feet (4,418 meters), the tallest mountain in the continental United States.

The hottest temperature ever recorded in North America, 134 degrees Fahrenheit (57 degrees Celsius), was chronicled in Death Valley on July 10, 1913. While hotter temperatures have possibly occurred elsewhere, it is just as probable that hotter temperatures have occurred here as well. Indeed, the *average* July temperature is 116 degrees Fahrenheit (47 degrees Celsius).

Located in the heart of the inhospitable **Mojave Desert**, Death Valley never had any permanent Native American settlements, but the nomadic Shoshone people did pass through. During the nineteenth century, prospectors came in search of

Badwater is 282 feet below sea level.

gold and silver, and their abandoned mines still dot the hills. The major mineral activity was borax, mined regionally in large quantities until after the turn of the twentieth century.

Death Valley National Monument, which includes the 57-mile (92-kilometer) valley floor that is entirely below sea level, was designated in 1933.

One of the famous 20-mule teams which once carried borax out of Death Valley.

22. DEVIL'S TOWER
Wyoming, USA

Monoliths, or gargantuan "single rocks," always have an otherworldly sense about them. They rise so abruptly from the relatively flat, surrounding terrain that it is almost like someone put them there, and for this reason, monolith legends abound. Australia is home to **Ayers Rock** (see no. 10), while the plains of Wyoming have **Devil's Tower**.

This strange phenomenon is an 865-foot (265-meter) tower of volcanically extruded, multi-sided columns. These columns were formed 50 million years ago in the same way as those at California's **Devil's Postpile** or Ireland's **Giant's Causeway** (see no. 29).

Like these other columnar formations, Devil's Tower is both surrounded by and named for a supernatural legend. The name was given by the Cheyenne people, who believed that the demon responsible for thunder lived here, and that the tower's star cluster, known as **The Pleiades**, was the remains of seven maidens who climbed the pinnacle to escape a bear. The tower's mysterious aura lived on into the twentieth century, when, in 1977, Steven Speilberg cast the monolith as a base for flying saucers in his film *Close Encounters of the Third Kind*.

Those having a close encounter with a successful climb to the top are treated to a magnificent view of five states, more than can be seen from the top of Manhattan's highest skyscraper.

Devil's Tower rises against the Wyoming sky.

23. DZUNGARIA
Xinjiang Uygur, China

Most of the Earth's surface is covered by water. Seen from space, our planet has been described at "the Blue Marble." Our vast oceans, lakes and rivers are basic to the reality of our existence. Mathematically predictable, but nevertheless puzzling, is that place on the Earth's solid surface that is the most remote from any of the world's great seas.

That place is in **Dzungaria** (the **Dzungarian Basin**), which is located in the Xinjiang Uygur Autonomous Region of far western China, near Kazakhstan's border. The Dzungarian Basin a dry, windswept place, where hearty souls tend to the herds of **bactrian camels** that are their means of contact with the outside world. And the outside world, as defined by contact with oceans, is far away.

Dzungaria is 1,645 miles (2,650 kilometers) from points on three great bodies of water, and the intervening land is anything but easily navigated terrain. To reach the

The bactrian camel.

frigid **Arctic Ocean** to the north, one must cross the breadth of Siberia. To reach the **Indian Ocean** to the south, one faces the **Tibetan Plateau** and the **Himalayas**. To the east, across the **Gobi Desert** and the breadth of China, lies the **Yellow Sea.**

A camel train crossing the Dzungarian Basin.

Few sights on Earth inspire more awe than that great peak in the **Himalayan Mountain Range**, once known to British surveyors as **Peak XV**, and still known in Tibetan folklore as "the mountain so high that a bird can't fly over it."

In Nepalese, the mountain is officially known as **Sagarmatha**; in Chinese, it is **Qomolangma**. To the rest of the world, it is known as **Mount Everest**, named for **Sir George Everest**, the head of the British India Company's Survey Department when the mountain was confirmed as the tallest on Earth.

In 1850, the mountain, which is on the border of Nepal and Tibet, was calculated to span 29,002 feet (8,840 meters) from ground to peak. However, in 1981, a satellite transit survey, in conjunction with a United States expedition to nearby **Mount Godwin Austen** (also known as **K2**), concluded that K2's peak, long held to be the world's second-highest, was actually 29,228 feet (8,909 meters), making it taller than Everest.

Since that time, more readings, possibly more accurate readings, have been taken using laser range finders and orbiting spacecraft. Although these readings don't agree, Everest is considered by most to be tallest. Most sources, including the 1994 *Oxford Encyclopedic World Atlas*, list Everest at 29,029 feet (8,848 meters) and K2 at 28,251 feet (8,611 meters). Meanwhile, the 1994 *Guinness Book of Records*, citing a 1987 ruling by the Research Council of Rome, lists Everest at 29,078 feet (8,863 meters) and K2 at 28,238 feet (8,607 meters).

Long considered unclimbable, Everest attracted an aura of foreboding from all the climbers who disappeared or died trying to scale it. The first successful attempt finally came after a climb of great difficulty, when **Edmund Hillary** of New Zealand and his Sherpa companion **Tenzing Norgay** reached the summit on May 29, 1953.

Since then, Everest has continued to claim the lives of mountaineers, but she has also been scaled numerous times. Without carrying oxygen, **Ang Rita Sherpa** climbed Everest seven times between 1983 and 1992, giving him the record for the most ascents by any one person. The first woman to reach the summit was **Junko Tabei** of Japan in 1975, and the first person to make the entire climb alone was **Reinhold Messner** of Italy in 1980.

Though she is known by many names, and has been measured many times with many different results, few who have gazed upon her frigid grandeur can disagree with her Tibetan appellation, **Goddess Mother of the World**.

Mount Everest.

The Everglades, located south of Florida's **Lake Okeechobee**, encompass about 7.5 million acres (three million hectares), nearly all of the state's southern area. They are a vast swampy area, described in the 1940s by conservationist **Marjory Stoneman Douglas** as "the River of Grass."

This amazing region is a landscape of waterways no more than six feet (two meters) deep, bisecting land whose elevation seldom rises above six feet (two meters). Mostly comprised of slough and swamp, the distinction between land and water is indistinct here. The Everglades are also home to a myriad of wildlife species, from the **wood stork**, **roseate spoonbill** and **osprey**, to the **Florida panther**, **manatee**, **crocodile** and **alligator.**

Yet this is a fragile ecosystem. In the early twentieth century, progress was defined as conquering the wilderness, and much of the Everglades was "reclaimed." Thankfully, in 1947, 1.5 million acres (610,000 hectares) were set aside as a national park, which also became a Biosphere Reserve in 1976. Since that time, an increased conservation awareness has helped preserve much of the remaining Everglades environment.

Nevertheless, Florida's expanding population has put tremendous pressure on fresh water reserves, reducing water levels and causing sea water to creep into the Everglades. According to the National Park Service, the wading bird population is only seven percent of the 1930 level, and the wood stork population is less than *one percent* of the 1960 level!

A classic image from the late 1800s, showing a riverboat moving slowly through the mysterious Everglades.

One of Asia's tallest mountains outside of the Tibetan plateau, **Mount Fuji (Fuji-san)** is remarkable for being an almost perfectly symmetrical cone-shaped volcano. As one of Japan's most important national symbols, it stands alone as the only natural feature — with the possible exception of Germany's **Rhine River** — that is regarded and revered as a unique emblem of its nation's identity.

Standing 12,388 feet (3,776 meters) above sea level, Fuji is 60 miles (100 kilometers) southwest of the Tokyo-Yokohama metropolitan area, making it visible on a clear day from many of Japan's most densely populated areas.

An inactive volcano, Fuji last erupted in 1707. It has been a popular subject in Japanese art for centuries, with the most famous depiction being the *Thirty-six Views of Mount Fuji*, a portfolio produced in 1835 by the great artist and printmaker **Katsushika Hokusai**.

Unlike the other great mountains of Asia, Fuji is not only easy to climb, but it is climbed by at least a quarter of a million people annually. Since 1868, these ranks have included women as well as men. The top of Mount Fuji is actually a volcanic caldera, 2,250 feet (685 meters) across, with eight specific peaks (known as petals) on its rim.

Mount Fuji Seen Below a Wave at Kanagawa,
from *Thirty-six Views of Mount Fuji.*
A color woodblock print by Katsushika Hokusai (1760-1849).

Tides are the regular, periodic rise and fall of the surface of all bodies of water, although they are most noticeable in oceans and seas because they are larger and more massive. Tides are caused primarily by the gravitational effects of the sun and moon. They vary from place to place, usually having a range between high and low tides of no more than ten feet (three meters). Indeed, there are only about a dozen places on Earth where the range is more than 20 feet (six meters).

While tides are principally effected by Earth's relation to the sun and moon, barometric pressure and wind effects can cause an extra "surge."

Due to a combination of factors, the greatest tides on Earth are found in the **Bay of Fundy** between Maine, New Brunswick and Nova Scotia. Here, in the spring, the average between high tide and low tide is 47.5 feet (14.5 meters).

According to the *Guinness Book of Records*, the highest tide ever recorded was 54.6 feet (16.7 meters) at **Ungava Bay**, Quebec in 1953. The lowest ocean tides are found on the **Pacific Ocean** island of **Tahiti**, where they are virtually nonexistent.

Grand Manan, an isolated island in the Bay of Fundy.

Among the world's great rivers, the **Amazon** and **Nile** vie for being the longest. The **Amazon** is certainly the one with the greatest water volume, but the **Ganges** has the distinction of being held as *sacred* by over 750 million Hindus worldwide. It is among the holiest of holies.

With headwaters — "the true source" — in an ice cave beneath **Gangotri Glacier** in the **Himalayas**, the Ganges also has the largest delta in the world. Spilling across parts of the Indian state of West Bengal and the nation of Bangladesh, this delta encompasses an area of 30,000 square miles (78,000 square kilometers).

From Gangotri, the water flows into the **Bhagirathi River**, which, in turn, merges with the **Alaknanda River** at **Devaprayag** in the Indian state of Uttar Pradish. At this point, the river becomes the Ganges proper, which flows 1,550 miles (2,500 kilometers) from here to the Bay of Bengal.

The Ganges flows through the **Siwalik Mountains** in an immense gorge, emerging at the sacred city of Hardwar, which every seven years becomes a destination for Hindu pilgrimages. Next, it flows down to Benares, the most sacred Hindu site and a bathing spot continually used by huge numbers of people. Benares is also important to Buddhists because it is here the Buddha first taught the Eightfold Path.

At the delta, which is still 220 miles (355 kilometers) from the bay, the Ganges merges with the great **Brahmaputra**, before entering the open water of the Indian Ocean.

An early twentieth century view of pilgrims bathing in the sacred Ganges River.

On the Atlantic coast of northern Ireland's County Antrim, there is a strange mass of nearly 40,000 six-sided, solid-stone columns, apparently hewn by human hands.

Crowded together along a section of shore 520 by 600 feet (160 by 180 meters), these pillars are mostly 18 inches (46 centimeters) across and stand at irregular heights, giving the impression of an elaborate staircase that might have been used by giants to disembark from their ships.

Because a similar "staircase" exists on an island off of Scotland, a legend developed that a mythological Irish hero, Finn MacCool, erected the pillars as part of a causeway to reach the island, which was home to a favored lady. Hence, County Antrim's mass has always been known as the **Giant's Causeway**.

In fact, the pillars were created during a primeval extrusion of molten basalt, which cracked with sudden, unusual and geometric precision. The shape, like that of a crystal, is related to the structure of basalt's individual molecules.

Such formations are rare but known elsewhere. There are some on the Scottish island of **Staffa**, and other, smaller sites on the County Antrim's coast. One, due to its overall shape, is known as the **Amphitheater**, while another is called the **Organ** because it looks like a pipe organ. There is even one in the United States, known as the **Devil's Postpile**.

Giant's Causeway in Northern Ireland.

THE GRAND CANYON
Arizona, USA

When one considers the world's greatest natural wonders, there are two that almost always come to mind instantly: **Mount Everest** in Asia and the **Grand Canyon** of the **Colorado River** in northwest Arizona.

One can imagine the shock of those who first discovered it, who were walking through pines and junipers and suddenly beheld a vast gorge a mile (1.6 kilometers) deep and spanning across for up to 18 miles (29 kilometers). These people may have been from the Havasupai or Navajo tribes, who have lived in the area for centuries. It was rediscovered by the Spanish in 1540. The first thorough geologic survey of the canyon — and possibly the first boat trip through it — was conducted by Major John Wesley Powell between 1869 and 1872.

The Grand Canyon is an almost unbelievable sight, so deep that it seems bottomless, so long that it seems endless. It is actually 277 miles (446 kilometers) long from **Marble Gorge** in the east to **Grand Wash Cliffs** in the west. Over the past five million years, the Colorado River has carved the Grand Canyon out of layers of sedimentary rock that average in age from five hundred million to two billion years.

The Grand Canyon was proclaimed as a National Monument in 1908, and it became Grand Canyon National Park in 1919.

An aerial view of the Grand Canyon.

Often the names that are given to wondrous natural features are quite literal. The **Grand Canyon** is such a name, and so is that of the **Great Barrier Reef**. Neither name does true justice. The Great Barrier Reef is just that: a reef that is a barrier. But it is more. A nearly solid wall of coral, it creates a nearly impenetrable barrier running for 1,260 miles (2,030 kilometers) along the continental shelf off the northeast coast of the Australian state of Queensland. (See map on page 43.)

On the east side of the Reef are the surging, crashing waters of the Coral Sea. To its west is a quiet blue-green sea that averages 50 miles (80 kilometers) in width.

The reef itself was constructed by trillions of coral polyps belonging to over 300 species, whose rock-hard and knife-sharp exoskeletons have formed this gargantuan mass over 100 centuries.

A close up of the coral and fish of the Great Barrier Reef.

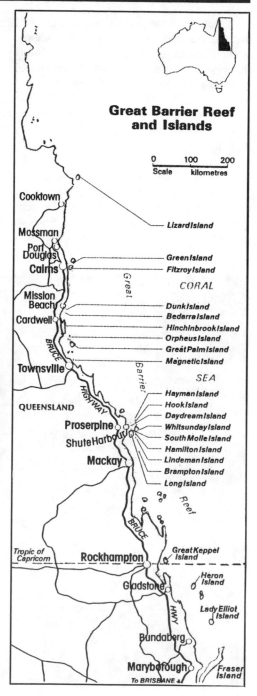

Great Barrier Reef and Islands

Scale 0 — 100 — 200 kilometres

Cooktown

Lizard Island

Mossman

Port Douglas

Cairns

Green Island

Fitzroy Island

CORAL

Mission Beach

Dunk Island

Cardwell

Bedarra Island

Hinchinbrook Island

Orpheus Island

Great Palm Island

Magnetic Island

Townsville

SEA

Hayman Island

QUEENSLAND

Hook Island

Daydream Island

Proserpine

Whitsunday Island

Shute Harbour

South Molle Island

Hamilton Island

Mackay

Lindeman Island

Brampton Island

Long Island

Reef

Tropic of Capricorn

Rockhampton

Great Keppel Island

Heron Island

Gladstone

Lady Elliot Island

Bundaberg

Maryborough

Fraser Island

To BRISBANE

In April 1992, the largest living thing on Earth was discovered in a Michigan forest. It was a 200,000-pound (91,000-kilogram) **monster mushroom fungus**, spreading underground across 40 acres (16 hectares). The most amazing thing about the great fungus was that something so immense had lain undiscovered until the last decade of the twentieth century.

Researchers confirmed that the fungus dates from 500 AD, and possibly earlier. Amazingly, it had existed in a heavily populated area without having been noticed or understood by humans for nearly fifteen centuries.

Called **Armillaria bulbosa**, fungi of this type inhabit tree roots and are known to exist in northern European and eastern North American forests, though none this large have been confirmed elsewhere. Other species of the **Armillaria** are found throughout the world, including the **honey mushroom** in California.

The fungus, scientists also said, is entirely living tissue, unlike the Sequoia's trees, whose bark is nonliving tissue. Testing of samples from the fungus showed researchers that each gene is identical. This convinced scientists that the organism is one gigantic living creature. Thus it can be concluded that the Armillaria is the biggest — and oldest — plant that ever lived.

The Great Fungus grows beneath the mossy surface of the Michigan forests.

North America's five **Great Lakes** have a total area of 73,800 square miles (191,000 square kilometers), making them the largest concentration of fresh water on Earth.

The largest of the five, **Lake Superior** (see no. 84), is the world's largest single body of fresh water, spanning 31,700 square miles (82,100 square kilometers). The others, in order, are: **Lake Huron** (23,000 square miles, 59,600 square kilometers), **Lake Michigan** (22,400 square miles, 58,000 square kilometers), **Lake Erie** (9,900 square miles, 25,600 square kilometers) and **Lake Ontario** (7,500 square miles, 19,500 square kilometers). After Africa's **Lake Victoria**, Huron and Michigan are the third- and fourth-largest bodies of fresh water on Earth.

All the Great Lakes border the United States and Canada, except Lake Michigan, which is entirely within the United States. The Great Lakes drain into the **Atlantic Ocean** via the **St. Lawrence River**.

Visited by **Etienne Brule** and **Samuel de Champlain** in about 1610, Lake Huron is possibly the first Great Lake seen by European explorers. It is 320 miles (515 kilo-meters) long, 118 miles (190 kilometers) wide and 750 feet (230 meters) deep at its deepest point. Its principal ports are London, Ontario and Bay City, Michigan.

Lake Michigan, explored in 1634 by **Jean Nicolet**, is 307 miles (494 kilometers) long, 118 miles (190 kilometers) wide and 870 feet (265 meters) deep at its deepest point. Its major ports are Chicago, Illinois; Milwaukee, Wisconsin; and Gary and South Bend, Indiana.

Lake Erie is 241 miles (388 kilometers) long and 57 miles (91 kilometers) wide, and has major ports in Cleveland, Ohio and Buffalo, New York. Lake Erie was the scene of an important Anglo-American naval battle during the War of 1812.

Lake Ontario is 193 miles (311 kilometers) long and 53 miles (85 kilometers) wide, and has major ports in Hamilton and Toronto, Ontario. Lake Ontario is the only Great Lake that does not freeze over in winter.

The Great Lakes are an important corridor for the shipping of grain, iron ore and manufactured goods. Detroit, Michigan, located between Lake Huron and Lake Erie, is the leading automobile manufacturing center in the world.

Until the mid-twentieth century, the lakes were important for their fisheries, but as industrial pollution had a considerable negative impact on the health of many species, fishing accordingly declined. Efforts to clean up the pollution reversed the trend by the 1980s, and today there is hope for recovery.

The **Great Salt Lake**, the world's second-saltiest body of water (after the smaller **Dead Sea** — see no. 20), is the largest American body of water after the Great Lakes (see no. 33). It is the remains of the long-extinct **Lake Bonneville**, a vast freshwater lake that was once 1,000 feet (300 meters) deep. Also a remnant of that prehistoric body of water is the nearby **Bonneville Salt Flats**, which have the distinction of being the flattest area on Earth.

Dried salt gathered into piles on the shore of the Great Salt Lake.

The Great Salt Lake is fed by the **Bear, Jordan** and **Weber rivers**, but has no outlet. It measures 75 miles (120 kilometers) north to south and 50 miles (80 kilometers) east to west. Dependent on evaporation for dissipation, its size has shrunk from 2,300 square miles (6,000 square kilometers) in 1873, to 1,078 square miles (2,792 square kilometers) in 1940, to 1,361 square miles (3,524 square kilometers) today. Large quantities of salt are still harvested commercially from the Great Salt Lake.

The region, explored by Jim Bridger in 1824, was selected by Brigham Young in 1847 to be a refuge for his Church of Jesus Christ of Latter Day Saints (Mormons). The rails of the Western Hemisphere's first transcontinental railroad were completed in 1869 at Promontory, which is within sight of the lake.

Young's original settlement has evolved into Salt Lake City, which is both the capital of Utah and the Mormon Church headquarters. Currently home to nearly 200,000 people, Salt Lake City remains the dominant religious and cultural influence in Utah.

A view of the Great Salt Lake, circa 1850.

The world's largest island, **Greenland**, is also the Northern Hemisphere's largest mass of ice on land. To put this in perspective, Greenland is three times larger than **New Guinea**, which is the world's second-largest island, and it contains 90 percent of all the Northern Hemisphere's ice on land. As a slab of ice, the **Greenland Ice Sheet** has no other rivals on Earth, except the **Antarctic Ice Sheet**.

Greenland has an area of 839,999 square miles (2,175,600 square kilometers) and 57,000 residents, making it less densely populated than Mongolia, the least densely populated independent country on Earth. The entire population lives in the capital, 16 small towns and 60 settlements. The remainder of the country is completely deserted.

The ice sheet itself averages 1,500 feet (5,000 meters) thick, while its winter temperatures average from -13 to -40 degrees Fahrenheit (-25 to -40 degrees Centigrade).

The first European to settle here was the Norseman **Eric the Red**, who named the decidedly white island "Greenland" in order to encourage other settlers. This was an early example of playing fast and loose with truth in advertising.

Today a self-governing possession of Denmark, Greenland could contain *50 Denmarks* within its area. When Greenland was a member of the European Economic Community (EC) from 1973 to 1985 (the people chose to withdraw), it constituted *half* of the EC's total land area.

The dog sled is still used as a means of transportation in Greenland.

We celebrate natural phenomena because they are natural, and hence superior to artificial or man-made wonders. As the great poet Joyce Kilmer intoned, "Poems are made by fools like me, but only God can make a tree."

On the other hand, we have a quirky fascination with natural objects that seem artificial, such as flowers whose color is too bright, as well as with natural objects that for a long time were considered to be made by either human hands or mankind's supernatural cousins, such as the **Giant's Causeway** (see no. 29) or the **Ritten** (see no. 76).

One of the strangest of such places is Australia's **Lake Hillier**. In the sparkling blue-green waters off Australia's south coast, there is a string of islands known as the **Recherche Archipelago**. They are dark green, wooded islands with rocky shorelines that have an occasional white sand beach. As you fly over them, they appear to be quite ordinary islands, until one reaches the simply named **Middle Island**, which is quite like the others, except that it contains Lake Hillier, which is far from being an ordinary lake. Located only a few yards from the deep blue waters of the **Australian Bight**, Hillier is a pink as a strawberry milk shake!

First discovered in 1802, Lake Hillier has always been a nearly opaque, brilliant pink — and very salty. Commercial salt production was attempted for a while, but the lake has been untouched for most of the twentieth century, as few people visit Middle Island.

The quite shallow Lake Hillier is about a mile (1.6 kilometers) long and about a third as wide. It was once thought that algae was responsible for its stunning coloration, but this was proven wrong, so its color remains a mystery.

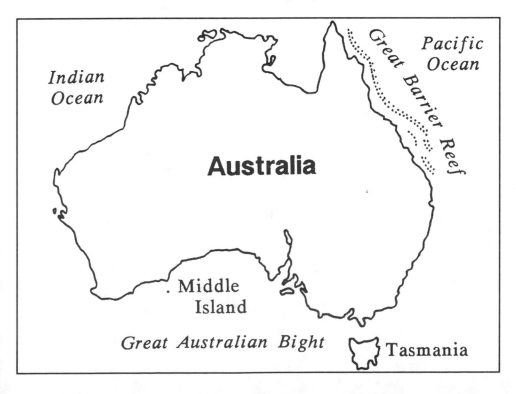

China's second-longest river, which is equal to the powerful **Yangtze** in terms of cultural importance to China, is the **Huang Ho (Hwang Ho)**, or **Yellow River**. The latter name is derived from the amount of yellow silt carried by the river. It is one of the world's mightiest rivers, draining an area of 600,000 square miles (1.6 million square kilometers) and spanning 4,840 miles (7,790 kilometers).

It originates in the highlands of Qinghai (Tsinghai) Province, flows eastward to the great lakes, **Gyaring Nor (Gyaring Hu)** and **Ngoring Nor (Ngoring Hu)**, and flows north through the Great Wall of China. The Yellow River then touches the edge of the **Gobi Desert** and turns south, where it forms the boundary between the Shaanxi and Shanxi provinces. It then flows through the breathtaking **Tungkwan Gorges**, the historic gateway to the sprawling **Wei Ho Valley**.

Turning eastward, the Huang Ho passes through the city of Jinan in Shandong Province before it enters the bay of **Bao Hai**, which is a thumb of the **Yellow Sea**.

Legendary for its great and violent floods, the Huang Ho brings life to a vast region, but it has also caused so many deaths that it has been referred to as "China's Sorrow." Indeed, it is so turbulent that it is recorded to have changed course over 1,500 times in 4,000 years.

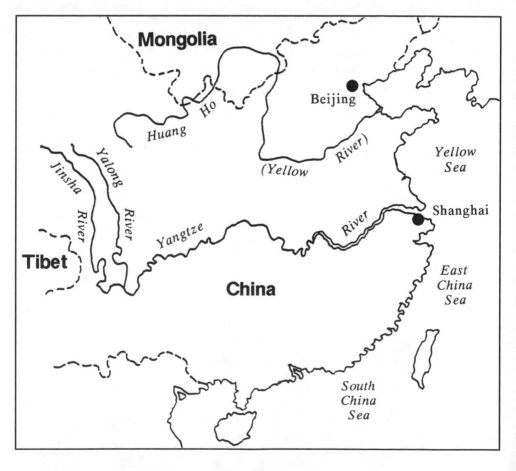

Among the fabled **Seven Wonders of the World** (as constructed by human hands), only one, the Pyramid complex at Giza in Egypt, still exists. The Hanging Gardens of Babylon and the Colossus of Rhodes are long gone. However, of Earth's myriad natural wonders, most will outlive all of us, all of our great grandchildren and probably our species.

On the other hand, the world's natural wonders include those that have completely vanished, like **Krakatoa** (see no. 46). Two others come to mind. We know about the great slabs of ice that cover the Arctic and Antarctic regions of the Earth, and how occasionally, pieces of this ice pack will break off to form **icebergs**, which drift by ocean currents to more temperate latitudes. Some of these are so big that they can endanger and even *sink* ships. The great Cunard Liner *Titanic*, sunk in April 1912, is a case in point.

While icebergs can be quite massive, only very rarely does their broadest dimension exceed a few miles or kilometers. An exception was the enormous **Ice Island T.1**, which was first seen adrift off Antarctica in 1946. It was estimated to be 200 feet (60 meters) thick and to have an area of 140 square miles (360 square kilometers). As we know, the larger the block of ice, the longer it takes to melt. Ice Island T.1 was so massive that it was still being observed in 1963!

Yet as big as it was, the legendary T.1 was eclipsed by the great **Ice Island of 1956**, an object so unusual that its description is almost like science fiction. Discovered in November 1956 near **Scott Island** in the South Pacific by the USS *Glacier*, this slab of ice measured 208 by 60 miles (335 by 100 kilometers) and had an area of 12,000 square miles (31,000 square kilometers), or large enough for the entire nation of Belgium to be laid upon it!

Icebergs in the South Pacific.

39. IGUAZU FALLS
Brazil/Argentina

South America's widest waterfall, **Iguazu (Iguassu) Falls**, is nearly three miles (five kilometers) wide, four times wider than **Niagara Falls** and **Victoria Falls** combined. Falling for 279 feet (85 meters), the thunder of the falls can be heard at distances up to 15 miles (24 kilometers).

Located on the **Iguazu River** at the Brazil-Argentina-Paraguay border, the falls are actually almost 300 small falls only a few feet (a few meters) apart. The highest of these is **Union Falls**, which spills into a gorge known as the **Devil's Throat**. In the rainy season, 58,000 tons (52,600 metric tons) of water are spilled per *second* from the **Parana Plateau**, from where it ultimately travels into the **Parana River**, 25 miles (40 kilometers) downstream.

Local legend holds that the falls were formed when a warrior named Taroba eloped with a chief's blind daughter, Naipur, who was also coveted by a local

A nineteenth century concept of South America's native population.

deity. He created the falls, turned Tardoba into a rock and threw him over. The deity then restored Naipur's sight, but turned her into a tree on the precipice to watch Taroba forever.

The first European to see the falls was **Alvar de Vaca**, who arrived here in 1541 and named them the **Salto de (Falls of) Santa Maria**.

The spectacular Falls of the Iguazu River.

The longest of the great rivers that begin in the **Himalayas**, the **Indus River** once (after 325 BC) formed the eastern border of Alexander the Great's empire. Today, however, it flows through the very heart of Pakistan. The Indus rises 17,000 feet (5,200 meters) into the glaciers of the Himalayan **Kailas Range**, which is close to the source of the **Brahmaputra River**, another of the Indian subcontinent's legendary waterways.

Flowing for 3,100 miles (5,000 kilometers) into the **Arabian Sea**, the Indus passes through some of the world's most rugged and beautiful country before it reaches the south of Peshawar, where it turns into a vast complex of many channels. During flood season, the Indus in northern Pakistan may become up to 25 miles (40 kilometers) wide.

Near Hyderabad, the Indus becomes the major source of **Lake Manchhar**, a strange marsh whose level rises and falls with that of the river. The Indus reaches the sea through a vast delta, which spans nearly 200 miles (300 kilometers) of the coastline south of the city of Karachi.

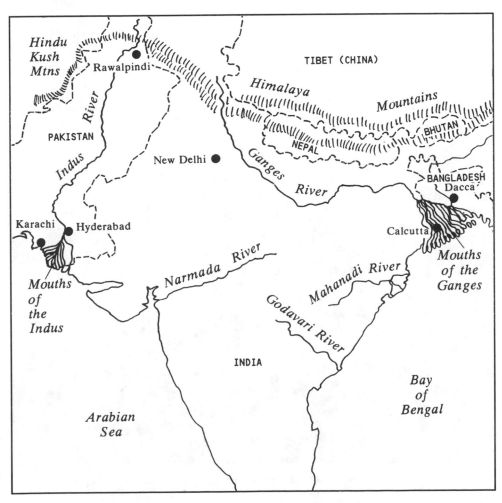

The **Kalahari Desert**, a sea of sand encompassing 200,000 square miles (518,000 square kilometers), spreads across virtually all of Botswana and touches Angola, Zimbabwe and Zaire. Since it is larger than any comparable area of the **Sahara Desert**, where the sand is interrupted by sections of gravel, the Kalahari is the world's largest concentration of pure sand.

A seemingly inhospitable place, the Kalahari is home to the **San** people, the Bushmen, whose culture is thought to have remained unchanged for 250 *centuries*. They survive by digging into the subsurface water table or underground streams.

The Kalahari is home to many species of snakes, antelopes and birds of prey. It also contains important archeological sites with Paleolithic art masterpieces.

Temperatures in the Kalahari rival those of the Sahara, often reaching 120 degrees Fahrenheit (50 degrees Celsius).

The African Elephant.

The water hole is where Africa's wildlife gathers, both predators and prey.

KILAUEA VOLCANO
Hawaii, USA

Kilauea Volcano, located on the southeast side of Hawaii, is certainly one of the world's most spectacular volcanos. While it doesn't soar to the amazing heights of Hawaii's other great volcanos, **Mauna Kea** and **Mauna Loa**, Kilauea is a cauldron of frequent, and often violent, activity, making it perhaps the most active volcano on Earth. Kilauea's longest rift-zone eruption in historical time began on January 3, 1983. A row of lava fountains broke out from its east rift zone about 11 miles (17 kilometers) from the summit caldera. Within a few months, the activity settled down to a single vent, but powerful fountaining episodes hurled molten rock 1475 feet (450 meters) into the air and built a cone of lava fragments that became the tallest landmark on the rift zone. The eruption changed its style abruptly in July 1986, when lava broke out through a new vent. Instead of regular episodes of high lava fountaining, lava spilled continuously onto Kilauea's surface. The steady outpouring of lava formed a molten rock lake that is perched atop a small shield volcano.

In June 1991, the shield was about 200 feet (60 meters) tall and 5,250 feet (1,600 meters) in diameter, while lava from the eruption covered 29 square miles (75 square kilometers) of forest and grassland, adding 300 acres (120 hectares) of new land to the island of Hawaii and destroying 179 homes in the process.

Today, most eruptions at Kilauea can be viewed at close range, but a few historical eruptions were dangerously explosive. Fast-moving mixtures of ash and gas, called pyroclastic surges, raced across the summit area and into the southwest rift zone during an

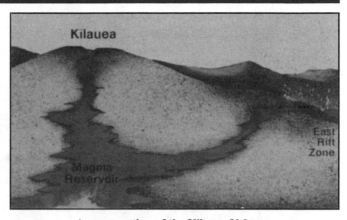

A cross section of the Kilauea Volcano.

eruption in 1790. Footprints preserved in a layer of ash 19 miles (30 kilometers) southwest of the summit probably include those of a party of Hawaiian warriors and their families, who were crossing the volcano when the eruption struck. An estimated 80 of the 250 fatalities were killed by the suffocating clouds that accompanied its pyroclastic surges.

A smaller explosive eruption in 1924, from Halemaumau Crater in Kilauea's summit caldera, killed a photographer who was too close and hurled rocks weighing as much as eight tons (seven metric tons) as far as half a mile (eight-tenths of a kilometer) away.

While most of Kilauea's historical rift eruptions were much briefer, prolonged eruptive activity in the east rift zone from 1969 to 1974 formed a similar shield, **Mauna Ulu** (Hawaiian for "Growing Mountain"), and an extensive lava field on the volcano's south flank. Geologic records reveal that such large-volume eruptions from the rift zones and summit areas, which cover large parts of Kilauea's surface, have occurred several times in the recent past. In fact, about 90 percent of Kilauea's surface is covered with lava flows that are less than 1,100 years old.

Straddling the border between two of east Africa's major states, and nearly straddling the equator, **Kilimanjaro** is the tallest mountain in Africa.

Actually it is a *pair* of volcanos with two peaks, the tallest of which, **Kibo**, stands 19,340 feet (5,895 meters) high. The smaller volcanic cone, **Mawensi**, is possibly extinct, while Kibo is categorized as a dormant volcano.

In ascending Kilimanjaro, one encounters several distinct climatic zones. The coffee and banana plantations that flourish in the hot equatorial environment at Kilimanjaro's base starkly contrast the summits of the two peaks that are always covered with snow.

Above: **The tallest mountain in Africa, Mount Kilamanjaro.**

Left: **An aerial view of the extinct volcano of Kibo.**

KINGS CANYON
California, USA

The **Grand Canyon** (see no. 30) is grand, a 277-mile (446- kilometer) gorge that is a mile (1.6 kilometers) deep and up to 13 miles (21 kilometers) wide. However, the deepest canyon in the world, as measured from the overlook's crest to the river at the gorge's bottom, is **Kings Canyon**, located on the **Kings River** in California.

Here, although the average depth of the canyon is the same as the Grand Canyon's steepest, the maximum distance from river bank to the top of the cliff is an incredible 1.6 miles (2.6 kilometers).

Kings River was originally named Rio de los Santos Reyes (River of the Holy Kings) by Gabriel Moraga, who found the canyon in 1806. After the site was visited by the great conservationist **John Muir** in 1873, efforts to preserve the area as a wilderness began. The canyon became a part of a federal entity known as the **Sierra Forest Reservation**, and in 1940, **Kings Canyon National Park** was established under joint administra-

tion with the adjacent **Sequoia National Park**.

Kings River flows west out of the **Sierra Nevada**, and the canyon's upper reaches are in Kings Canyon National Park. The canyon continues beyond the park to form the boundary between the **Sequoia National Forest** and the **Sierra National Forest**.

A spectacular aerial of Kings Canyon.

This is not an important river for its length, width or long history of civilizations along its shores. The **Klondike River** is, however, uniquely legendary: mile for mile, the gravel that formed the bed and banks of the Klondike was richer in pure gold nuggets than any of the world's other rivers.

Barely 100 miles (160 kilometers) long, the Klondike is a minor tributary of the **Yukon River**. It is fed by streams, such as **Bonanza Creek** and **Eldorado Creek**, whose names bear witness to the amazing Klondike gold rush that began with the dis-

covery of the yellow metal here on August 17, 1896.

The population of the town of Dawson, situated where the Klondike flows into the Yukon, grew from about 100 to more than 20,000 by 1898. The gold discovered during a single season of the rush's 1900 peak would be worth $6.75 billion today!

By 1910, the rich place had been exhausted and the rush was long past. In the late 1930s and during World War II, new discoveries brought the Klondike gold fields back to life, but only briefly. Today the period of the Klondike gold rush is recalled for having produced numerous masterpieces of adventure literature that were penned by such renowned storytellers as **Jack London** and **Robert Service**.

Left: **Chilkoot Pass during the Klondike Gold Rush.**
Below: **Miners sitting on their supplies.**
"At 3 o'clock this morning the steamship Portland, from St. Michaels for Seattle, passed up [Puget] Sound with more than a ton of solid gold on board and 68 passengers."
(July 17, 1897 *The Seattle Post-Intelligencer***)**

At 9:00 a.m., local time, on August 27, 1883, **Krakatoa** was merely one of many uninhabited, though volcanically active, islands in the straights between Java and Sumatra in what is now Indonesia. An hour later, Krakatoa exploded with a force of 1,482 megatons, 26 times greater than the largest hydrogen bomb ever detonated.

The largest explosion to take place on Earth in modern history and the second-largest in recorded history (see no. 80, **San-torini**), the Krakatoa eruption threw debris 34 miles (55 kilometers) into the air and killed 36,380 people through its blast and resulting tidal wave.

Debris fell for ten days over a vast area up to 3,313 miles (5,331 kilometers) away, and the blast was heard over an area larger than the continent of Africa. It is said that the sky lit up as far away as Europe and North America, and that the ash in the atmosphere caused vivid, ruddy sunsets for three years.

An artist's concept of the Krakatoa explosion.

Modern cities are criss-crossed by miles and miles of streets, boulevards and freeways, all surfaced with asphalt. Imagine a place in the heart of a major American city where the bodies of long-extinct **saber-toothed tigers** (*smilodons*) from the **Pleistocene** epoch lie preserved in asphalt.

These cats, along with wolves, birds of prey and their prey, were discovered in Southern California at what was once the **Rancho La Brea**, but what is now in the heart of Los Angeles. Specifically, the remains are immersed in sticky, naturally occurring asphalt ooze where the animals fell more than 10,000 years ago.

The **La Brea Tar Pits** have yielded a wealth of information about the **Ice Age's** animal and plant life, and more discoveries are being made still as paleontologists dig through the tar's gooey mass.

The pits are open to the public, and the adjacent **George C. Page Museum** hold numerous examples of the discoveries made here.

Above: The saber-toothed tiger was often caught in the same tar pits where its intended dinner was trapped.

Left: This painting of a saber-toothed tiger is based upon the fossilized remains found in tar pits.

Europe's largest lake is so large that Europe's six smallest nations could *all* fit within it as islands 50 miles (80 kilometers) from its shoreline. Encompassing an area of 7,100 square miles (18,400 square kilometers), **Lake Ladoga** is 130 miles (210 kilometers) long and 80 miles (130 kilometers) wide.

Many of the world's lakes are covered with ice in winter, and some even freeze so solid that trucks can use them as icy highways. In the case of Lake Ladoga, the ice actually saved one of the world's greatest cities. From 1941 to 1944, during World War II, German armies surrounded the city of Leningrad (known before 1917 and since 1991 as St. Petersburg), which lies at the southwestern corner of Lake Ladoga. The Germans cut the city off from the rest of the then-Soviet Union, and it was only through the use of truck convoys across the ice that the city's people survived the three terrible winters of the siege.

Lake Ladoga is fed by 70 major rivers, with its outflow going to the **Neva River**, which flows into the Gulf of Finland. The ice forms in October or November, and usually breaks up in March, but the lake may remain ice-bound until June.

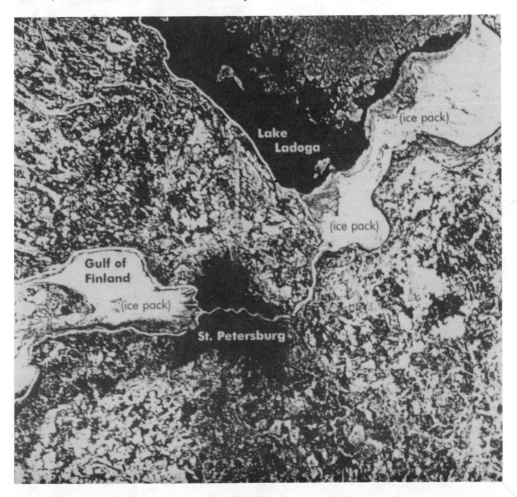

Long before the 1980 eruption of **Mount St. Helens**, a series of spectacular eruptions from **Lassen Peak** between 1914 and 1917 demonstrated the explosive potential of the volcanos of the **Cascade Range**. Small explosions began on May 30, 1914, and were followed during the next 12 months by more than 150 explosions that sent clouds of ash as high as two miles (three kilometers) above the peak. The activity changed character in May 1915, when a lava flow was observed in the summit crater.

A deep red glow from the hot lava was visible at night 21 miles (34 kilometers) away. On May 19, the lava spilled an avalanche of hot rocks onto the snow and triggered a mud flow that travelled more than nine miles (15 kilometers) away from the volcano. The most destructive explosion occurred on May 21st, when a pyroclastic flow devastated forests as far as four miles (6.5 kilometers) northeast of the summit, and mud flows swept down several valleys radiating from the volcano.

An enormous ash plume rose more than six miles (nine kilometers) above the peak, and prevailing winds then scattered the ash as far as 310 miles (500 kilometers) eastward across Nevada. Lassen Peak continued to produce smaller eruptions until about the middle of 1917. The site, which was declared as the Lassen Peak & Cinder Cone National Monument in 1906, became Lassen Volcanic National Park in 1916.

Above: **The Painted Dunes.**
Below: **The ash cloud from the May 22, 1915 eruption of Lassen Peak**

50. LONG VALLEY CALDERA
California, USA

Vast yet unseen, the ominous **Long Valley Caldera** lies on the eastern front of the **Sierra Nevada** mountain range, about 185 miles (300 kilometers) east of San Francisco. A huge explosive eruption about 700,000 years ago formed the caldera and produced pyroclastic flows that traveled 40 miles (65 kilometers) from the vent and covered an area of about 600 square miles (1,500 square kilometers).

Ash from the caldera-forming eruption fell as far east as Nebraska, but within the past 40,000 years, eruptions have been restricted to a linear zone of vents, including the **Mono-Inyo Craters Volcanic Chain**, which extends about 20 miles (50 kilometers) north from the northwest part of the caldera.

This volcanic chain consists of many vents that have erupted in the past several thousand years. Eruptions from vents as recently as 550 years ago produced lava flows, pyroclastic flows and ash. Geologic mapping shows that some eruptions were preceded by ground cracking, suggesting that the ground was pulled apart or stretched as magma neared the surface.

Three moderate earthquakes occurred south of the caldera, and one beneath the caldera, on May 25th and 26th in 1980, marking the beginning of a period of unrest that would continue into the 1990s. Swarms of earthquakes beneath the caldera, changes in several hot springs, and the formation of new springs have occurred since 1980. Precise surveys have also shown that the central part of the caldera has risen by more than 20 inches (50 centimeters) since 1975. This unrest is probably related to both the stretching (east-west extension) of the Earth's crust, which is known to be occurring around the caldera, as well as the rise of magma beneath the caldera.

Scientists do not know if this unrest will lead to volcanic activity, but the geologically recent eruptions along the Mono-Inyo Craters Volcanic Chain suggest that future eruptions are possible.

An aerial view of the Mono-Inyo Craters Volcanic Chain.

Caves and underground chambers fascinate us for many reasons. Maybe it's because they are like another world, a parallel universe, unseen and unknown, yet so very near and so real.

In 1799, a hunter chasing a bear through the hills near Kentucky's **Green River** literally stumbled into what has turned out to be the most extensive such parallel universe yet to be found. This hunter was not the first to explore **Mammoth Cave**, but he probably was the first in 4,000 years, and he certainly was the first of many that came to snoop over the next 200 years.

Concerts were held in the underground chambers; Edwin Booth, the actor brother of the man who shot Abraham Lincoln, performed in plays here; nitrate for gunpowder to fight the War of 1812 was mined here; tuberculosis patients were treated here; and cave explorers died terrible deaths here. Such is the mystique of this wild wonderland of snow white, gypsum columns and colorful stalactites and stalagmites.

Hollowed out by millions of years of the action of water on limestone, Mammoth Cave has 348 miles (560 kilometers) of *explored* chambers and an unknown length that has not been seen by human eyes yet.

Set aside as a National Park in 1941, this labyrinthine cave system contains fast-moving underground rivers, such as the **Echo River** and the **River Styx,** that are filled with blind fish. **Mammoth Dome** is a room 192 feet (59 meters) high, and the **Bottomless Pit** has a bottom, but it is as deep as a ten-story elevator shaft and most flashlight beams cannot reach its bottom.

Above: Stalactites, stalagmites and other cave formations.
Left: The Ruins of Karnak, giant water-carved limestone columns, in Mammoth Dome.

Though the distinction of being the tallest mountain in Europe belongs to 15,771-foot (4,807-meter) **Mont Blanc** in the **French Alps**, Europe's most famous — and indeed, most visually striking — peak is the **Matterhorn**. A 14,691-foot (4,478-meter) mountain in the **Swiss Alps**, the Matterhorn's shoulders are in the **Italian Alps**, where it is known as **Monte Cervino**, after its first surveyor, Servius Galba, who was a consul to Julius Caesar.

Immortalized in every medium from paintings to postcards to chocolate wrappers, the Matterhorn has a nearly pointed tip and sharply defined ridges that outline cirques, or circular basins, carved by ancient glaciers.

Because of its incredibly sharp, steep sides, the Matterhorn had been written off as unclimbable since before the time of Servius. **Horace Bénédict de Saussure**, who had already conquered Mont Blanc said, "Its precipitous sides, which give no hold to the very snows, are such as to afford no means of access."

In 1865, a party led by English climber **Edward Whymper** reached the top from the Swiss side, long thought to be the steepest. Though thousands of climbers have conquered the Matterhorn since then, the treacherous cliffs still claim a dozen or so lives annually.

The Matterhorn.

On an island where spectacular sights are almost commonplace, one is most uncommon. The highest mountain on Earth in terms of its altitude above sea level is **Mount Everest** (see no. 24) in the **Himalayas**. The highest mountain on Earth in terms of its distance from the center of the Earth is **Chimborazo** (see no. 17) in the **Andes**. The highest mountain on Earth in terms of its height from its base is **Mauna Kea** on the island of Hawaii.

Mauna Kea's peak is 13,796 feet (4,205 meters) above sea level, but while Everest — 29,238 feet (8,912 meters) above sea level — rises about 14,000 feet (4,300 meters) above the **Qinghai-Tibet Plateau**, Mauna Kea rises 33,480 feet (10,200 meters) above its base on the floor of the Pacific Ocean.

Its name in Hawaiian means "White Mountain," for even on a tropical island such as Hawaii, Mauna Kea is perpetually snow-covered, and indeed it even is possible to go skiing on its slopes.

A dormant — but hardly extinct — volcano, Mauna Kea is the highest point in the state of Hawaii, and because it is also relatively isolated from city lights, it is perhaps world's most perfect site for astronomical observatories. Located atop it are the 148-inch (376-centimeter) United Kingdom Infrared Telescope (UKIRT), the 142-inch (361-centimeter) Canada-France-Hawaii Telescope and the 118-inch (300-centimeter) NASA Infrared Telescope.

A Landsat view of Hawaii and its volcanoes.

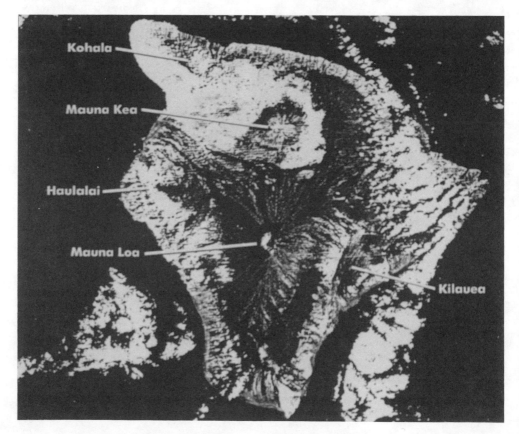

Kohala

Mauna Kea

Haulalai

Mauna Loa

Kilauea

Located immediately south of the great **Mauna Kea** on the island of Hawaii is her awesome sister, **Mauna Loa**. Standing 13,678 feet (4,169 meters) above sea level, Mauna Loa rises 33,362 feet (10,169 meters) above the ocean floor, making her also over twice as high in base to peak as **Mount Everest**.

Unlike Mauna Kea, however, Mauna Loa is a still-active volcano, one of the world's largest active volcanos. It has erupted 15 times in the twentieth century, with eruptions lasting from less than a day to as many as 145 days.

The most recent eruption began before dawn on March 25, 1984. Brilliant lava fountains lit the nighttime sky as fissures opened across the floor of the caldera. Within hours, the summit activity stopped and lava began erupting from a series of vents along the northeast rift zone. When the eruption stopped three weeks later, lava flows were only four miles (6.5 kilometers) from buildings in the city of Hilo.

Mauna Loa erupts less frequently than Kilauea, but it produces a much greater volume of lava over a shorter period of time.

Lava fountains erupting from Mauna Loa's rift zone.

Today bearing the name of William McKinley, the 25th United States president, the tallest mountain in North America was traditionally known to Native Americans as **Denali**, which in the Athabascan language means "the High One."

William McKinley, who had this wonder named for him while he was a senator, was assassinated in 1901, so he never actually saw it. In 1917, the mountain and its surrounding area were set aside as **Mount McKinley National Park**, but when the park's boundaries were expanded in 1980, it was renamed **Denali National Park**.

While Mount McKinley stands 20,320 feet (6,194 meters) tall, the vertical rise of 18,000 feet (5,500 meters) from the nearby valley floor is greater than any mountain in the world, including **Mount Everest** (see no. 24). McKinley's lower second peak stands 19,470 feet (5,930 meters) high, which would make it North America's second-highest peak if it were a separate mountain.

McKinley is part of the 600-mile (1,000-kilometer) **Alaska Range**, which formed 65 million years ago as a result of activity along the **Denali Fault**, North America's largest. Earthquakes still rumble in the Denali region and geologists believe that the mountain is still getting higher. McKinley is always snow-covered, and nearly a dozen major glaciers creep outward from its slopes, the longest of which is the 50-mile-long (80-kilometer-long) **Kahiltna Glacier**.

Above: **A timber wolf.**
Below: **Majestic Mount McKinley, covered by its permanent snow fields.**

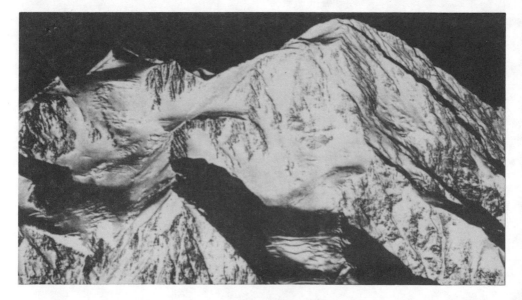

No rainstorms experienced on a regular basis in temperate climates can compare to the tropical **monsoon**. It is to the downpour what the downpour is to the sprinkle.

In the temperate world, Denver gets an annual average of 15 inches (38 cm), Honolulu gets 22 inches (56 cm), London gets 23 inches (58 cm), Chicago gets 33 inches (84 cm), Sydney gets 46 inches (117 cm) and Vancouver, in the notoriously rainy Northwest, gets 60 inches (152 cm).

In areas where monsoons are prevalent, the situation is quite magnified. Dacca in Bangladesh gets an annual average of 105 inches (267 centimeters), while Freetown in Sierra Leone gets 175 inches (445 centimeters).

This pales by comparison to the state of **Meghalaya** in India, which holds the record for the wettest place on Earth. The annual rainfall average here is an incredible 467.5 inches (1,187.5 centimeters). The greatest recorded annual rainfall, which was in the town of Cherrapunji in Meghalaya, was 1,041.8 inches (2,646.2 centimeters). Cherrapunji's record month exceeds the five-year total for most of the wettest places in the temperate world: 366 inches (930 centimeters)!

A classic engraving of the elephants of India.

57. MISSISSIPPI RIVER
United States

Renowned in myth and legend as "the Father of Waters," the **Mississippi River**, the second-longest river in North America, is the major component in the 3,710-mile (5,970-kilometer) **Mississippi-Missouri-Red River System**, which is often regarded as the third-longest river in the world. Even more significant is the fact that the Mississippi and its tributaries have an area of drainage that encompasses over one million square miles (2.6 million square kilometers), 40 percent of the United States.

The Mississippi itself originates in **Lake Itasca**, in northern Minnesota, and runs for 2,350 miles (3,800 kilometers), reaching the **Gulf of Mexico** through the vast **Mississippi Delta** below New Orleans. The river is easily navigable and has been an important transportation route for America's midsection since the French colonial period in the eighteenth century.

Its major tributaries are: the **Ohio River**, which flows into the Mississippi at Cairo, Illinois; the **Missouri River**, which flows into the Mississippi at St. Louis, Missouri; the **Arkansas River**, which flows into the Mississippi between Memphis, Tennessee and Natchez, Mississippi; and the **Red River**, which flows into the Mississippi near Natchez.

Some of the great masterpieces of American literature have been set on the Mississippi River. These include *Huckleberry Finn* and *Tom Sawyer*, written by **Mark Twain (Samuel Clemens)**, who was himself a river boatman in the late nineteenth century and took his pen name from a riverboat depth-sounding term.

The Mississippi River as a key transportation corridor was an important element in the strategy of both sides during the American Civil War. General Ulysses S. Grant's defeat of the Confederate forces at Vicksburg, overlooking the river, is seen as a key milestone in the eventual Union victory.

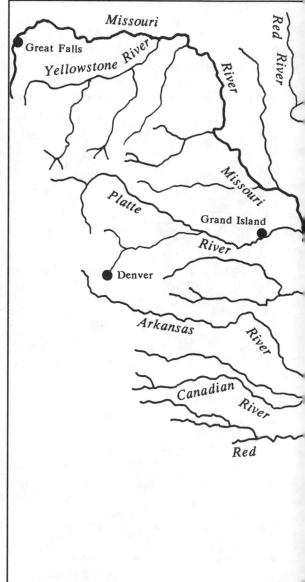

The **Missouri River** is the longest river in North America and a key component in the 3,710-mile (5,970-kilometer) **Mississippi-Missouri-Red River System**, which is often regarded as the third-longest river in the world.

The Missouri itself originates in the confluence of the **Madison, Gallatin** and **Jefferson rivers** in western Montana and drains an area of 529,000 square miles (1,370,000 square kilometers). It flows for 2,714 miles (4,368 kilometers), meeting the **Mississippi River** in St. Louis, Missouri.

Its major tributaries include the **Yellowstone River**, which flows into the Missouri near the Montana-North Dakota border, and the **Platte River**, which flows into the Missouri at Omaha, Nebraska.

Though not as important a transportation corridor as the Mississippi, the Missouri, navigable for much of its length, was the principal route taken by Meriwether Lewis and William Clark in their epic expedition of the Louisiana Purchase in 1804-1806. A series of huge dams, completed since the 1930s, provide hydroelectric power as well as water for both irrigation and local municipal use in Montana, Nebraska and the Dakotas.

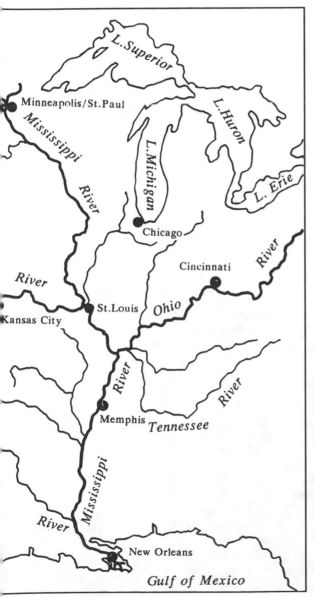

Vicksburg, Mississippi, one of the many towns along the banks of both the Missouri and Mississippi rivers.

In County Clare, where Ireland faces the stormy **North Atlantic Ocean**, there is an incredible line of great limestone cliffs that rise abruptly from the ocean. Here, a person standing on the plateau above can look straight down into the foaming sea from a distance equivalent to the height of 40 to 70 story buildings!

This line of cliffs runs across the Atlantic faces of both Clare and the off-shore **Aran Islands**, which stand like sentinels in the mouth of **Galway Bay**. The most impressive segment is the front in west Clare, ten miles (16 kilometers) wide, that is known as the **Cliffs of Moher**.

The cliffs are named for the ancient fort of Mothair, one of many fortifications that were built along the crest by the Celtic people in about 500 BC. Though Mothair was destroyed long ago, well-preserved ancient forts still exist on the Aran Islands. With the cliffs themselves forming a formidable natural defensive line, the practical reason for these forts remains a mystery.

Inland from the Cliffs of Moher is a vast limestone plateau known as the **Burren**. It contains numerous caves, including the extensive complex known as the **Aillwee Caves**, which were inhabited in Neolithic times. Though the Burren seems barren and is treeless, nearly 80 percent of all the plant species found in Ireland can be found here.

The cliffs of Moher.

There is a remote basin (Mark Twain called it "the loneliest place on Earth") located on the east side of the Sierra Nevada that is on the way to nowhere. Within this basin is a lake that is literally on the way to nowhere. By this we mean there is no outflow except evaporation, and that through evaporation, the lake will ultimately disappear.

Mono Lake is 700,000 years old and was originally much larger than its present 60 square miles (155 square kilometers). As the lake has shrunk, it has become saltier. Now three times saltier than ocean water, it long ago ceased to support the fish that once lived here, and its increasing salinity threatens the brine shrimp that once thrived here.

This is a strange environment, indeed, one of the strangest in North America. Here, the waters team with fly larvae, and light slabs of volcanic rock float in the thick, salty water. Its islands are covered with steaming vents of hot springs and frozen, white forests of **tufa**, which are spindly spires of calcium carbonate that were formed on the lake's bottom when it was deeper.

The ancient Shoshone people once lived on these shores and gave the lake its name, Mono, which means brine flies. The first Europeans to see the lake were the party of trappers who were led by **Joseph Walker** and stumbled upon it in 1833. The area is now protected as part of the **Mono Basin National Forest**.

A view across the waters of Mono Lake.

In this book, we have spoken of islands that no longer exist, like **Santorini** (see no. 80), and atmospheric phenomena that few have seen and no one can really explain. We also have spoken of a **Great Fungus** in Michigan that went undetected for hundreds of years.

In California, there is something that may or may not exist, but upon whose existence hundreds of thousands of people have bet their lives and fortunes. If this natural wonder *does* exist, it would be worth almost any cost.

On January 19, 1848, James Marshall discovered a piece of shiny, yellow metal in some gravel in the stream at Sutter's Mill in the **Sierra Nevada's** California foothills. It was not so much that Marshall found gold — because a great deal of gold had already been found in the West — but that people soon discovered that there was quite a lot of it, and it was close to the surface, not in a deep mine.

During 1848, the trickle of prospectors staking claims in the Sierra Nevada turned into a river. In 1849, the river became a deluge, and the California gold rush quickly turned into the biggest voluntary migration in recent human history. Many people became very rich, and few became fabulously wealthy.

The Gold Rush lasted less than a decade, but the search continues to this day, with often positive, but usually negative results. Throughout the years, especially in that first decade after 1849, prospectors spoke of the mystical and perhaps mythical **Mother Lode**. Literally, it is the mother of all the smaller deposits that were found. Large nuggets and indeed huge nuggets were found, such as the one weighing 195 pounds (90 kilograms) that was found in Calaveras County in 1854. But the Mother Lode was never located.

It is imagined to be a vein of gold of vast dimensions, perhaps equal to all the gold yet discovered everywhere in the world since the beginning of history. Perhaps it is many times that size, and perhaps it does not exist.

The search continues, and while it has not been found, it has not been for lack of trying.

An 1886 engraving of the archetypical prospector, always searching for the big strike, following every rumor and tall tale of the Mother Lode.

NAMIB DESERT
Namibia

We take it for granted that coastlines in the temperate regions of the world are among the most settled, inhabited and "tamed" places on Earth. However, the coastline of the African nation of Namibia (Southwest Africa until 1968 and fully independent since 1990) is not. While many coastlines have sandy beaches, and even sand dunes, the Namibia coast has the **Namib Desert**, a sandy beach that is 30 to 50 miles (50 to 80 kilometers) across! This vast, desolate desert runs along the length of this 800-mile (1,300-kilometer) coastline. With the exception of the port at Walvis Bay, the Namib is largely uninhabited. Even most of the rivers that flow from its interior dry up before they reach the coast.

The 300-mile (500-kilometer) stretch of coast north of Walvis Bay is known as "the Coast of Hell," or "the Skeleton Coast." This is because a unique confluence of difficult ocean currents and high winds make the waters offshore as inhospitable as the desert, and the coastline is littered with hundreds of ships to prove it. Indeed, these maritime corpses include everything from small fishing boats to huge passenger liners. In 1942, when the *Dunedin Star* ran aground here, it took a month to rescue its passengers and crew.

The Skeleton Coast mystery is accentuated by the discovery of a dozen headless skeletons and their effects that had lain in the coastal dunes for nearly a century.

A sailing ship foundering on the shores of the Skeleton Coast.

63. NIAGARA FALLS
Canada/USA

North America's most famous waterfall, **Niagara Falls**, is actually two waterfalls separated by **Goat Island**. The **American Falls** and the **Horseshoe (Canadian) Falls** are located adjacent to one another on the 35-mile (56-kilometer) **Niagara River**, which forms the border between New York State and the Province of Ontario. While they appear about the same size, Horseshoe Falls carries 94 percent of the water, or 36,000 cubic feet (1,000 cubic meters) per second.

Between them, they are three-fourths of a mile (1.2 kilometers) wide and 167 feet (51 meters) high. While not the tallest falls in North America, the sight — and sound — of two vast, continuous sheets of water make them one of the most spectacular. Formed in the **Quaternary Ice Age Period**, when the Niagara River changed course due to being blocked by glacier debris, the falls are relatively new, geologically speaking.

First seen by Europeans about 1683, the falls have been a major tourist attraction ever since, especially since the mid-nineteenth century, when road and rail connections made the site convenient to visitors from population centers such as Montreal, Philadelphia, Toronto and New York City. Stunts, such as riding over the falls in a barrel, have always been common, and

Niagara Falls.

have caused frequent fatalities. The great tightrope-walker **Charles Blondin (Jean Francois Gravelet)** has successfully crossed the falls various times, including on a tightrope, on stilts, blindfolded, carrying another man and pushing a wheelbarrow.

An aerial view of the American Falls on the left and Horseshoe Falls on the right.

The **Nile River** (in Arabic, **Nahr En Nil**), which is the world's longest river, is 4,160 miles (6,695 kilometers) from its source in the **Kagera River**, which flows into **Lake Victoria**, to its outlet through Egypt's **Nile Delta** into the **Mediterranean Sea**.

From Lake Victoria, the Nile flows through **Lake Kyoga** and **Lake Albert**. There, because of its white-water rapids, the Nile is known as the **Victoria Nile** or the **White Nile**. At Khartoum in the Sudan, the White Nile is joined by the **Blue Nile**, whose headwaters are in Ethiopia. From there, the Nile flows north into Egypt. The source of the Blue Nile was discovered in a 1770-1772 expedition by **James Bruce**, while the source of the White Nile was traced by various people, including the great Anglo-American explorer **Sir Henry Stanley**, in the 1880s.

Flowing through Egypt, the Nile brings life to the **Sahara Desert** because it makes irrigation possible. It was upon its Egyptian shores that one of the ancient world's greatest cultures developed. Beginning in about 3200 BC, and reaching its apogee around 1200 BC, the civilization of ancient Egypt was perhaps the richest and most complex the world had yet seen, in terms of factors ranging from the sciences to its monumental achievements in architecture that still survive today. And all of this because the valley of the Nile supported a concentrated population so well and for so long.

Overlooking the Nile in the **Valley of The Kings** in southern Egypt are breathtaking ancient ruins in such legendary sites as Luxor, Karnak and Abu Simbel.

During the twentieth century, two major dams, the **Aswan Dam** (1902) and the **Aswan High Dam** (1971), were constructed for irrigation and hydroelectric purposes across the Nile in southern Egypt. A massive effort undertaken by the United Nations relocated the great Temple of Abu Simbel to save it from inundation by the Aswan High Dam.

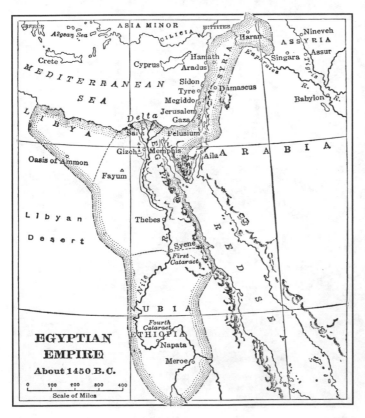

EGYPTIAN EMPIRE

About 1450 B.C.

0 100 200 300 400

Scale of Miles

NOHOCH NA CHICH
Mexico

As we know, caves hold a fascination for us because they are so mysterious. When we are walking, we can usually see our destination in the distance. Caves, on the other hand, lead to places that we cannot see. There is a surprise at every turn. Much also can be said about the underwater world. To combine the two is to journey to **Nohoch Na Chich** in Quintana Roo.

Located in Mexico, Quintana Roo is the home to Nohoch Na Chich, a labyrinthine network of underwater caves. Exploration of this strange world was undertaken in 1987, and within seven years, 70,087 feet (21,363 meters) of passageways had been mapped, but there is still more to be explored.

With this, Nohoch Na Chich is by far the longest underwater cavern system known to exist in the world.

One of the passageways within Nohoch Na Chich.

The world's largest volcanic eruption during the twentieth century occurred in June of 1912 at **Novarupta** on the Alaska Peninsula. An estimated 530,000 cubic feet (15,000 cubic meters) of magma explosively erupted for 60 hours. To put this into perspective, it was about 30 times the volume erupted by Washington's **Mount St. Helens** in 1980!

The expulsion of such a large volume of magma excavated a funnel-shaped vent 1.2 miles (two kilometers) wide and triggered the collapse of the **Mount Katmai** volcano six miles (ten kilometers) away, forming a summit caldera 2,000 feet (600 meters) deep and about 1.8 miles (three kilometers) across. Extrusion of the lava dome, now called Novarupta, near the center of the 1912 vent marked the eruption's end.

Until a scientific expedition sponsored by the National Geographic Society visited the area four years later, almost nothing was known about the spectacular effects of this great eruption. To their amazement, scientists found a broad valley northwest of Novarupta marked by a flat plain of loose, sandy ash material from which thousands of jets of steam were hissing. The eruption had

The Katmai National Park and Reserve also protects Alaska's brown bear.

produced pyroclastic flows that swept about 13 miles (21 kilometers) down the upper **Ukak River valley**. The thickness of the resulting pumice and ash deposits in the upper valley is not known, but they may be as great as 660 feet (200 meters). In 1916, the deposits were still hot enough to boil water and form countless steaming fumaroles. From that day, this part of the Ukak River has been known as the **Valley of Ten Thousand Smokes**.

The area was set aside in 1918 as **Katmai National Monument**, which in turn became a national park in 1980.

The steaming vents of Novarupta Volcano.

The world's great deltas, such as those of the **Nile, Amazon** and **Indus rivers**, are monumental wonders, spilling vast volumes of water into the **Mediterranean, Atlantic** and **Indian oceans**. Not all great deltas spill their water into seas and oceans. North of the arid and parched **Kalahari Desert**, which is the world's largest expanse of open sand dunes, lies the world's largest delta that leads nowhere.

The **Okavango River** flows from the **Cubango River**, which forms the border between Angola and Namibia, to Botswana, where it forms the great **Okavango Delta**, a vast network of waterways 50 miles (80 kilometers) long and ten miles (16 kilometers) wide. However, these don't lead into a great body of water, but into oblivion.

In years of heavy precipitation, the Okavango Delta can swell to 8,500 square miles (22,000 square kilometers), with thousands of **hippopotamuses** and **crocodiles** swimming half-submerged. But as it flows on to the south, the fingers of the delta grow narrower and shallower, and then they are gone. The millions of tons of water all evaporate in the 120 degree Fahrenheit (50 degree Celsius) heat of the Kalahari, so the delta simply vanishes into sand.

A hippopotamus in the Okavango Delta.

The biggest thing on the Earth's surface and our largest ocean is the vast **Pacific Ocean**. Accounting for 45.9 percent of the world's surface area, it encompasses 64.2 million square miles (166 million square kilometers) and has an average depth of 13,740 feet (4200 meters).

The shortest continent-to-continent navigable distance across the Pacific is the 10,905-mile (17,550-kilometer) path from Bangkok, Thailand in Asia to Guayaquil, Ecuador in South America.

The Pacific Ocean contains the deepest point on the floor of any of the world's oceans, the **Challenger Deep** (see no. 16), which is located in the **Marinas Trench** in the western Pacific Ocean 170 nautical miles (275 kilometers) south of Guam.

Also within the Pacific are the great sea mountains **Mauna Kea** (see no. 53) and **Mauna Loa** (see no. 54), which are taller from base to summit than any other mountain on Earth. Underlying the Pacific Ocean is the great **Pacific Plate**, one of the great segments of the Earth's crust. Surrounding both the ocean and the plate is the ominous **Ring of Fire** (see no. 75), which is literally a ring that virtually runs around their entire 35,000-mile (57,000-kilometer) circumference. It contains over half of the world's active and potentially active volcanos as well as most of the world's active earthquake faults.

Excluding Greenland, Madagascar, Baffin Island and the continent of Australia (which touches the Pacific and the **Indian Ocean**), the Pacific is the location of the world's largest islands, including New Guinea, Borneo, Sumatra and the islands that make up Japan. The thousands of other islands — many of them tiny — that exist in the Pacific are organized into vast archipelagos or watery "continents" that are larger from edge to edge than Europe, but have less land area than Luxembourg. These include Micronesia, Melanesia, Polynesia and the Hawaiian archipelago.

The *Golden Hind*, the first British ship on the Pacific Ocean.

The **Pripet (Pripyat) Marshes**, which are Europe's largest swamp, cover an area of 18,000 square miles (47,000 square kilometers), an area larger than the Netherlands and Luxembourg combined. Located in western Russia and Belarus, they are in the basin of the **Pripet River**, one of the tributaries of the **Dnieper River**.

The basin, known locally as **Polesye**, is 150 miles (240 kilometers) wide and 300 miles (500 kilometers) long, but in spring, flooding can extend it many miles or kilometers. The front of the ice sheet during the Ice Age lay just to the north, and the streams of melt-water deposited great quantities of material, especially sand, and thus helped to choke the drainage.

Most of the area consists of marshlands of reeds, bulrushes and grasses, with an occasional peat bog. Dry "islands" are heavily wooded. Attempts to drain the swamps date back to 1872 and have been marginally successful in turning small tracts into fields for flax or potatoes.

Tragically, the nuclear explosion at Chernobyl in 1986 has contaminated much of the marshes with radiation fallout and no one knows what long term ecological effects this will have upon the Pripet.

Above: **The Kingfisher is a common marsh bird throughout Europe.**
Below: **The ancient ice sheet.**

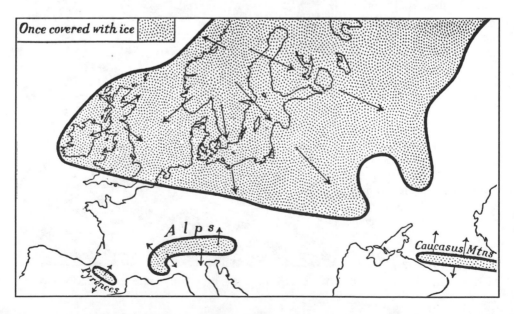

Once covered with ice

Alps

Pyrenees

Caucasus Mtns

We take it for granted that the land we walk upon is older than our oldest ancestor, older even than our species. The phrase "old as the hills," implies that something — or someone — is old beyond measure. We assume that even the youngest of hills is tens of thousands — if not hundreds of thousands — of years old. Mostly we are right to assume this — but not always.

Through volcanic action, our Earth is always creating new land, and even new bodies of land, such as the islands formed during the twentieth century off Iceland and around the Pacific Ocean's **Ring of Fire** (see no. 75).

Earth's newest body of land, named **Pulau Batu Hairan** or Surprise Rock, is located in the **South China Sea**, where it sits 40 miles (65 kilometers) northeast of Kudat in Sabah, Malaysia.

Born in 1988, Pulau Batu Hairan has an area of just two acres (four-fifths of a hectare) and an elevation, depending on the tides, of barely ten feet (about three meters). It is not presently inhabited.

Sea gulls on Pulau Batu Hairan, or Surprise Rock.

Mount Rainier, standing 14,409 feet (4,392 meters) high, is one of the tallest mountains in the **Cascade Range**. Visible from downtown Seattle, its perpetually snow-capped peak is a striking sight. Though it has not produced a significant eruption in the past 500 years, scientists consider it one of the most hazardous volcanos in the Cascades.

The largest single-peak glacier system in the United States, Rainier has 26 glaciers which contain more than five times as much snow and ice as all the other Cascade volcanos combined. If only a small part of this ice were melted by volcanic activity, it would yield enough water to trigger enormous mud slides.

Mount Rainier's potential for generating destructive mud flows is enhanced by its great height above the surrounding valleys and its "soft" interior. The volcano stands about 9,900 feet (3,000 meters) above the river valleys leading from its base. Volcanic heat and groundwater have turned some of the volcano's originally hard lava into soft clay minerals, thereby weakening its internal structure. These conditions make Mount Rainier extremely susceptible to large landslides. Several of these have occurred in the past few thousand years, while the most recent one happened about 600 years ago. These landslides, apparently containing great volumes of water, quickly turned into mud as they rushed down river valleys.

In 1899, 235,000 acres (950 square kilometers), which include the peak and its surrounding area, were established as Mount Rainier National Park.

Mount Rainier.

Perhaps the most active and violent volcano in North America, Alaska's **Mount Redoubt** erupted four times in the twentieth century. The most recent eruption was on December 14, 1989, three months after a major earthquake on the **San Andreas Fault** (see no. 79) in California. Following several days of strong explosive activity, a series of lava domes grew in Redoubt's summit crater during the following four months. Most of the domes were destroyed by explosions or collapsed on the volcano's north flank.

Some of these events triggered small flows that melted snow and ice on the volcano, forming mud flows in the **Drift River Valley**, which empties into the Cook Inlet 20 miles (35 kilometers) away. Ash produced by the eruptions severely affected air traffic en route to Anchorage, Alaska's largest city and a major hub of domestic and international commercial air traffic. Many domestic airlines suspended service to Alaska following these major explosive events, and several international carriers temporarily re-routed flights around Alaska. On December 15th, a jetliner en route to Japan encountered an ash cloud while descending into Anchorage. The plane quickly lost power in all four engines and lost 13,100 feet (4,000 meters) in altitude before the pilots were able to restart the engines. The aircraft landed safely in Anchorage, but it sustained more than $80 million in damage.

Mount Augustine, a neighboring and very active volcano, has a symmetrical cone that rises 4,114 feet (1,254 meters) above sea level. Since Captain James Cook discovered and named it in 1778, Augustine erupted in 1812, 1883, 1935, 1963, 1976 and 1986. Curiously, the quiet intervals between eruptions apparently have shortened from 70 to ten years. The 1986 eruption began with eight months of earthquake activity beneath the volcano and a violent explosion. Billowing ash plumes rose more than six miles (ten kilometers) above the vent, and ash spread throughout the Cook Inlet area. Soon lava began erupting near the volcano's summit and added about 80 feet (25 meters) to the top of the existing lava dome. Small pyroclastic flows accompanied the growth of the dome.

In the 1883 eruption, part of the volcano's summit collapsed into the sea. Within an hour, a **tsunami** (tidal wave) as high as 30 feet (9 meters) crashed ashore 50 miles (80 kilometers) away on the coast of the **Kenai Peninsula** .

Redoubt Volcano erupting on December 16, 1989.

RED SPRITES and BLUE JETS
High in the atmosphere

Within the realm of unexplained natural phenomena, few have been more mysterious and controversial than the strange blobs of light that are known as **red sprites** and **blue jets**. Observed for many years by pilots of high altitude aircraft above violent thunderstorms, none were successfully videotaped until 1989.

These ghostly tongues of light are typically found in the **mesosphere** and the **thermosphere**, 20 miles (32 kilometers) or more above the Earth's surface. The blue jets appear as flashes that look like lightning or electrical sparks. The red sprites can be as tall as 40 miles (65 kilometers) and resemble angels, cauliflowers or octopuses, which have several long tentacles.

These phenomena are not common, but during one 67-minute period in the summer of 1994, 97 sprites were observed over Colorado and Kansas.

Though they have been observed and measured, they have yet to be explained. They are probably electrical discharges of some kind, but no one really knows exactly what they are. Physics professor John Winkler of the University of Minnesota, who has observed and photographed sprites, believes that "every explanation has holes in it. We're in on the beginning of a new aspect of science."

An artist's concept of red sprites.

This great river, which figures so prominently in German legends and history, has its source in Switzerland and its mouth in the Netherlands. The **Rhine River** has two main sources, the **Vorder Rhein,** which flows from **Lake Toma**, and the **Hinter Rhein**, which flows from the base of the **Rheinwaldhorn** in the **Adula Alps**. They join at Reichenau, flow past Chur, and briefly form an Austrian border before passing through **Lake Constance (Bodensee)** on the German border.

At Schaffhausen, the river flows across the spectacular **Falls of the Rhine** and then to the city of Basel, which is the furthest point upstream where the Rhine is navigable. Downstream from Basel, the river leaves Switzerland, forming a 175-mile (300-kilometer) border between Germany and France's Alsace region before solely becoming a German river.

From Mainz, where the **Main River** flows into the Rhine from the east, to Koblenz, where the **Moselle (Mosel) River** flows into the Rhine from the west, the Rhine passes through the deep gorge formed by the **Taunus** and **Rhenish mountains**. The steep hillsides are covered with vineyards and studded with medieval castles and forts, which were used through the turbulent Middle Ages and beyond as headquarters for feudal lords, who collected high tariffs on commercial shipping.

It is this section of the Rhein which figures so prominently in classical German mythology. Among the stories is that of the **Lorelei,** a rock near St. Goar that was home to a beautiful siren, whose haunting song lured sailors to their deaths.

The Rhine continues through mountainous country between Koblenz and Bonn, the capital of West Germany after 1949 and the administrative capital of Germany after its unification. Downstream from Bonn, the Rhine flows through the lowlands and the Ruhr region, Germany's great industrial heartland. At the border of the Netherlands, the Rhine splits into two parallel rivers, the **Lek** to the north and the **Waal** to the south. The former flows through Rotterdam to reach the **North Sea** at Hoek van Holland, while the latter flows into a great, sprawling delta before reaching the North Sea.

Historic Rheinstein Castle overlooking the Rhine River in Germany, circa 1910.

More than simply an allusion to a country song by Johnny Cash, the Earth's own **Ring of Fire** is one of its most striking natural features as well as one of its largest. It is literally a ring that runs virtually the entire 35,000-mile (56,000-kilometer) circumference of the **Pacific Plate**, which underlies the **Pacific Ocean**. It is almost literally "on fire," for over half of the world's active and potentially active volcanos are on the Ring of Fire, as are most of the world's active earthquake faults.

Most volcanos form long mountain ranges and are concentrated on the edges of continents, along island chains or beneath the sea. According to the theory of **plate tectonics**, the Earth's crust is made up of a patchwork of about eight large and seven smaller plates that move relative to one another at speeds ranging from less than half an inch (one centimeter) to about an inch (2.5 centimeters) per year. This is roughly equal to the speed at which fingernails grow. These rigid plates, whose average thickness is about 50 miles (80 kilometers), are spreading apart, sliding past each other, or colliding with each other in slow motion on top of the Earth's hot, pliable interior. Volcanos tend to form where plates collide or spread apart, although they can also grow in the middle of a plate, like the Hawaiian volcanos do.

The ocean floor is spreading apart and forming new ocean crust along this valley, or "rift," as hot magma from the Earth's interior is injected into the ridge and erupts at its top. In the Pacific Northwest, the **Juan de Fuca Plate** plunges beneath the **North American Plate**. As the denser plate of oceanic crust is forced deep into the Earth's interior beneath the continental plate, a process known as subduction, it encounters high temperatures and pressures that partially melt solid rock. Some of this newly formed magma rises toward the Earth's surface to erupt, forming a chain of volcanos above the subduction zone.

There are high concentrations of volcanos in Japan, the Aleutian Islands, Indonesia, the United States and New Zealand, as well as on the South American Coast. Some major recent eruptions on the Ring of Fire have included **Mount Pinatubo** in the Philippines (1991), **Mount Augustine** off the Alaskan Coast (1986), **Nevado del Ruiz** in Columbia (1985), **El Chinchonel** in Mexico (1982) and **Mount St. Helens** in Washington (1980).

Major earthquakes — exceeding 6.6 on the **Richter Scale** — have occurred recently along the Ring of Fire near Kobe in Japan (1995), near Los Angeles (1994), near San Francisco (1989), near Mexico City (1985), in Guatemala (1976) and in the Philippines (1976).

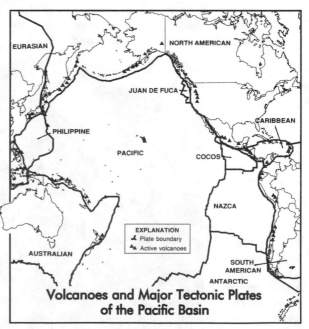

Volcanoes and Major Tectonic Plates of the Pacific Basin

Imagine walking through the woods and suddenly coming upon a group of spindly stone pillars that are a yard wide at the base and taller than the surrounding trees — and each one has a boulder twice its own diameter balanced on its peak!

And yes, the boulders are really separate from the columns. They are even a different kind of rock!

Such are the strange formations known in German as **Ritten**, in Italian as **Renon** and in French as **Demoiselles Coiffees** (young ladies with hats). They are located throughout the foothills of the **Alps** at an elevation of roughly 3,200 feet (1,000 meters), though a particularly high concentration is found in the South Tyrol region that was once part of Austria but is now part of Italy.

Wherever they are found, the Ritten have long been the subject of folk tales and legends, usually involving the supernatural beings that put the boulders atop the pillars.

In fact, the Ritten were not placed on their pillars by giants or fairy folk, but were created when thick mudstone was deposited at the end of the Ice Age and gradually turned to soft stone. Lying atop and mixed into this material were hard igneous boulders. Over succeeding centuries, rain pouring down washed away all of the soft mudstone, except that protected by boulders lying atop it. As hard as it would seem to have happened this way, the boulders protected many columns higher than 100 feet (30 meters) from being washed away by the rain. Similar features exist in the American Southwest, but they are usually entirely made of sandstone.

The strange and wonderful Ritten.

The world's largest desert, the **Sahara**, encompasses an area of 3.5 million square miles (9.1 million square kilometers) that stretches across North Africa from the **Atlantic Ocean** to the shores of the **Red Sea**.

It is a dry and barren place, composed of sand, gravel and rock. Occasionally an **oasis,** a tiny freshwater spring, exists with a cluster of palm trees around it, but for the most part, the Sahara Desert is a vast, almost uninterrupted ocean of lifeless sand dunes. It is crossed on land by only the heartiest of traders and travelers with their **dromedary (one-humped) camels**, or,

more recently, four-wheel-drive vehicles, whose drivers have plenty of containers of extra water.

The Sahara is also the hottest place on Earth, with average annual temperatures above 70 degrees Fahrenheit (20 degrees Celsius). The hottest temperature ever recorded on Earth was 136 degrees Fahrenheit (58 degrees Celsius) in the shade at **Al'Azizia**, Libya on September 13, 1922.

The most desolate region within the Sahara is probably the **Tenere Desert**, the California-sized "desert within a desert" on the border of Niger, Chad and Libya.

A camel caravan traveling across the vast and desolate Sahara.

North America's most famous recently-active volcano experienced a catastrophic eruption on May 18th, 1980. This was preceded by two months of intense activity, which included more than 10,000 earthquakes, hundreds of small steam-blast explosions and the outward growth of the volcano's entire north flank by more than 260 feet (80 meters). A magnitude 5.1 earthquake that struck beneath **Mount St. Helens** at 8:32 a.m. on May 18th set the devastating eruption in motion.

Within seconds of the earthquake, the volcano's bulging north flank slid away in the *largest landslide in recorded history*, triggering a destructive, lethal and lateral blast of hot gas, steam and rock debris that swept across the landscape as fast as 680 mph (1,100 kph). Temperatures within the blast reached as high as 575 degrees Fahrenheit (300 degrees Celsius). Snow and ice on the volcano melted, forming torrents of water and rock debris that swept down the river valleys leading from the volcano. Within minutes, a massive plume of ash rose 12 miles (19 kilometers) into the sky. The prevailing wind then carried about 490 tons (445 metric tons) of the ash across 22,000 square miles (57,000 square kilometers) of the western United States.

After the eruption, more than a dozen extrusions of thick, pasty lava built a mound-shaped lava dome in the new crater. The dome is about 3,600 feet (1,100 meters) in diameter and 820 feet (250 meters) high. The event dramatically illustrated the type of volcanic activity and destruction that **Cascade Range** volcanos can produce. In contrast to Hawaii's **Kilauea** (see no. 42), Cascade volcanos erupt a variety of magma types that generate a wide range of eruptive behavior and build steep-sided cones, which are known as composite volcanos. During such eruptions, magma is shattered into tiny fragments (chiefly ash and pumice) and ejected thousands of feet or meters into the atmosphere or even the stratosphere. Under the force of gravity, sometimes these fragments sweep down a volcano's flanks at high speeds, mixing with air and volcanic gases to form pyroclastic flows.

Mount St. Helens towers over the massive landslide caused by the earthquake and volcanic eruption of May 18, 1980.

There is probably no natural feature in the United States whose name conjures up more fear and dread than California's **San Andreas Earthquake Fault** (see map on page 51). And as often is the case, the fears are more myth than reality. While many of the serious earthquakes which have occurred in the continental United States' recorded history have been centered on the San Andreas Fault, most of the damage was caused by ancillary events, such as fires. Furthermore, many states in the east and southeast — certainly including Florida — have suffered far more damage from hurricanes than California has from San Andreas' earthquakes.

The Earth's crust is made up of a patchwork of plates that move relative to one another at speeds ranging from less than a half-inch (one centimeter) to about an inch (2.5 centimeters) a year. Occasionally, the plates suddenly slip violently, travelling distances of several feet (up to about a meter). Earthquake faults are located parallel to and along the plates' borders. Specifically, the San Andreas Fault is an especially long fault — running most of California's length — and is one of many that are located parallel to where the **Pacific Plate** and the **North American Plate** meet (see map on page 82).

Another well-spread myth is that an earthquake on the San Andreas Fault would cause California to fall into the **Pacific Ocean**. This is impossible because except for a few small slivers, all of California is located on the North American plate.

While earthquakes occur in California annually, few cause ma-

A fence offset over eight feet by the fault line.

jor damage, and many are not actually on the San Andreas Fault.

In the twentieth century, the San Francisco Bay Area (the fault actually bypasses San Francisco's city limits) was struck in 1906 by a magnitude 8.3 earthquake, which left over 500 people dead, and in 1989 by a magnitude 7.1 quake, which caused 67 fatalities.

While both of these were San Andreas earthquakes, the notorious 1971 (6.5) and 1994 (6.6) quakes in the San Fernando Valley, north of Los Angeles, were on adjacent faults, the latter occurring on a fault line that was previously unknown.

Buckled pavement and the city in ruins after the 1906 earthquake.

The volcano of **Santorini** on the island of Thera once occupied a corner of the Aegean Sea about 60 miles (100 kilometers) north of Crete. As has been reconstructed from ancient records, its annihilation in 1628 BC was the largest explosion to take place on Earth in recorded history. The entire central part of the island collapsed, destroying the city of Akrotiri. It is now believed that this event is the source of the Plato's story about the destruction of Atlantis.

Indeed, it was three times the size of the August 27th, 1883 explosion on the island of **Krakatoa**. The size of the Santorini explosion has been estimated at roughly 4400 megatons, which is 78 times greater than the force of the largest hydrogen bomb ever detonated.

The Santorini eruption probably sprayed debris 100 miles (160 kilometers) into the air and possibly even into orbit in outer space. The death toll is not known, but if Krakatoa killed 36,380 people through its blast and resulting tidal wave, Santorini may have caused up to 100,000 fatalities, as the Greek Islands were fairly densely populated in 1628 BC.

Debris would certainly have fallen in Egypt and Mesopotamia, and possibly as far away as India and France. The blast would have been heard throughout Europe, much of Africa and China.

Modern Santorini is a circle of islands which are actually the rim of the flooded crater. A new volcanic cone has appeared in the lagoon and the beautiful city may someday be destroyed again.

A view of modern Santorini with the rim of the flooded caldera in the background.

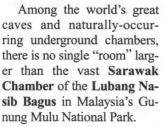

Among the world's great caves and naturally-occurring underground chambers, there is no single "room" larger than the vast **Sarawak Chamber** of the **Lubang Nasib Bagus** in Malaysia's Gunung Mulu National Park.

When the chamber was discovered, it was large enough to defy belief, so in 1980, a British-Malaysian survey team eliminated some of the disbelief by measuring it. The Sarawak Chamber is so vast that New York City's Madison Square Garden is claustrophobic by comparison, while Houston's Astrodome would easily fit inside.

With a length of 2,300 feet (700 meters) and a width of 980 feet (300 meters), it is large enough to contain at least two dozen football fields!

From floor to ceiling, the Sarawak Chamber is more than 230 feet (70 meters), easily high enough to contain a 20-story skyscraper. On the floor of the chamber are house-sized boulders which the explorers mistook for walls.

An artist's concept of the Sarawak Chamber's limestone formations.

There are land masses with pockets of water called lakes, and there are great bodies of water with isolated pieces of land called islands. Then there is the strange **Sargasso Sea**, a sea within an ocean that is actually like a swamp that should exist on land.

Located in the **Atlantic Ocean** northwest of the West Indies, the Sargasso Sea is a vast bog of seaweed that encompasses an area of two million square miles (five million square kilometers), an area nearly ten times larger than the **Caspian Sea** and all of North America's **Great Lakes** combined.

Known to mariners since the time of Christopher Columbus in the late fifteenth century, the Sargasso Sea is often impenetrable by ships. The seaweed itself, which is of the species *Sargassum natans* and *Sargassum fluitans*, comprises a vast plant community that circulates with the current and is unconnected to any solid surfaces.

The fate a seaman dreads, becalmed in the Sargasso Sea.

As a species, California's great **Sequoia** or **Redwood** trees are the world's largest living things. There are two distinct types, the Sequoia (*Sequoia dendron giganteum*), which is found in Central California's **Sierra Nevada** range, and the **Coast Redwood** (*Sequoia sempervirens)*, which is found within 50 miles (80 kilometers) of the Pacific Ocean between the Monterey Peninsula and the Oregon border.

The Sequoias are generally larger in diameter and volume, while the slender Coast Redwoods are usually taller. Indeed, the tree recognized as the world's *tallest* is a Coast Redwood, which stands 367.8 feet (112.1 meters) tall and is located in **Redwood National Park** in California's Humboldt County. The tallest Sequoia stands 311 feet (95 meters).

The world's *largest* tree is "the General Sherman," a Sequoia located in **Sequoia National Park** in Tulare County. Still growing, it currently stands a "mere" 275 feet (85 meters), but its trunk has a circumference of 103 feet (31 meters). The tree weighs an estimated 2.8 million pounds (1.3 million kilograms).

While there are Coast Redwoods that have been determined to be 2,000 years old, Sequoias have been dated at 3,200 years of age, and "the General Sherman" may have sprouted as early as 700 BC.

Ironically, the seeds from which both trees grow are tiny, no bigger than tomato seeds. While the Sequoia grows only from seeds, the Coast Redwood may *also* reproduce by sprouting from existing roots. DNA tests on closely-spaced trees have shown that all the trees in a grove may actually be clones of a single "parent."

Big Trees in Mariposa Grove.

The largest body of fresh water on Earth, **Lake Superior** is one of North America's five **Great Lakes** (see no. 33). Second only to the salty **Caspian Sea** (see no. 15) among the world's biggest lakes, Lake Superior covers 31,700 square miles (82,100 square kilometers).

Located in a depression in the Canadian shield, Lake Superior is fed by 200 rivers, draining an area of 80,900 square miles (209,500 square kilometers). Like all of the Great Lakes except **Lake Michigan**, which is entirely within the United States, Lake Superior is on the border between the United States and Canada. It flows into **Lake Huron** at Sault Sainte Marie, a city that straddles the border between the two countries. In addition to this city, the major ports on Lake Superior are Duluth, Minnesota; Superior, Wisconsin; and Thunder Bay, Ontario.

The largest island in the lake is **Isle Royal**, which became a United States National Park in 1931.

Etienne Brule was the first European to visit the lake, but the native Ojibwa and Menominee people lived there for centuries before his 1623 arrival.

Today, Lake Superior is important for shipping minerals and agricultural products, as well as for fishing, as **trout**, **whitefish** and **sturgeon** abound in its waters.

Above: Isle Royal.
Right: An aerial view of the American canal and locks at Sault St. Marie, circa 1940.
Below: Pictured Rocks National Lakeshore.

THE TEPUIS
Venezuela

Imagine a jungle so thick that it is effectively impossible to traverse it on foot. Imagine that this jungle spreads out like a vast, undulating sea as far as your eyes can see. Now imagine that there are huge, steep-sided islands that thrust up from this sea. What you are imagining is a reality in southeast Venezuela, where huge plateaus, called **tepuis**, are literally like islands that rise up hundreds of feet or meters above the surrounding rain forests.

The amazing thing about these 100-some plateaus is that their sides are so high and so steep that most are unclimbable. Indeed, they are literally separate worlds. Indeed, only a handful of people have even set foot on them. Even helicopters are hard to use because of violent down-drafts.

After English botanist **Everard Thurn** climbed the one known as **Roraima** in 1884, he stunned the world with reports of plant species that were unknown elsewhere. This fact inspired **Sir Arthur Conan Doyle** to pause from penning his Sherlock Holmes stories to write *The Lost World*, a tale of adventurers who travelled to one of these plateaus and found it inhabited by strange tribes of humans, sub-humans and dinosaurs!

While it is not possible that dinosaurs would have been able to survive for millions of years, subsequent expeditions have confirmed that roughly 5,000 species — from toads to varieties of orchids — are found only on various tepuis.

Above and right:
The tepuis of Venezuela.

Any natural reaction — whether it is a seed germinating or yeast causing bread to rise — depends upon conditions being just right. The same is true of human civilization, which can itself be considered a part of natural evolution. Among the world's great river valleys, one has the distinction of being the place where conditions were naturally right for the dawn of human civilization.

Human beings first began making tools and developing organized societies 30,000 years ago in many parts of the world, but it was about 8,000 years ago that humans first began building elaborate, permanent cities and developing systems of government based on written law. In order for this to happen, humans first had to resolve the problems of a steady, consistent food supply, and this had to occur in an environment where people could focus on establishing a civilization, not protecting themselves from the weather.

The place where all these conditions were present was the valley of the **Tigris** and **Euphrates rivers**, known to history as both the **Fertile Crescent** and the **Cradle of Civilization**. Among the great cities that once flourished here were Ur and Babylon. Today, Baghdad, Iraq's capital, is the most important city in the region.

The Euphrates (in Arabic, Nahr al Furai) is the longest river in western Asia. It flows roughly 1,700 miles (2,700 kilometers) from the western highlands of Turkish Armenia to a great Delta, known as the **Shatt al Arab**, at the head of the Persian Gulf.

The Tigris (in Arabic, Nahr Dijah) originates in Turkey's **Lake Golcuk** and flows for 1,150 miles (1,850 kilometers) before it joins the Euphrates about 100 miles (160 kilometers) from the Persian Gulf. For most of their length, the two rivers are less than 150 miles (240 kilometers) apart, and the region between them contains a large-scale, systematic irrigation project that is the world's oldest.

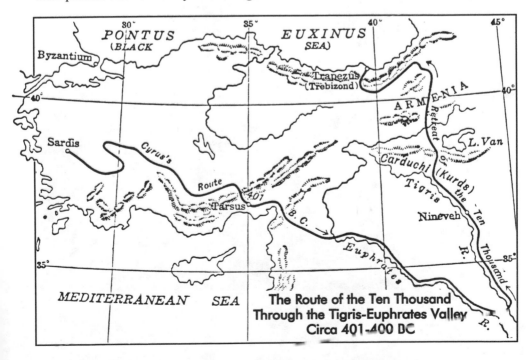

The Route of the Ten Thousand Through the Tigris-Euphrates Valley Circa 401-400 BC

Situated mainly in Peru but having a corner in Bolivia, **Lake Titicaca** is the largest lake in South America's **Andes** and the *highest* navigable lake in the world. Located at an elevation of 12,506 feet (3,812 meters), Titicaca has an area of 3,200 square miles (8,290 square kilometers) and measures 110 miles (177 kilometers) long and 35 miles (56 kilometers) wide. On its surface, steamers run between Guaqui, Bolivia and Puno, Peru.

The lake is fed by myriad streams that flow from the surrounding Andes. Its outflow is via the **Desaguadero River**, which terminates in the salty **Lake Poopo**, where it evaporates.

Titicaca is 1,558 feet (475 meters) deep, and there are rumors of "lost gold" thrown onto its bottom by ancient Incas, either as part of a ritual sacrifice or to keep it out of the hands of the invading Spanish in the sixteenth century. With the Spanish came Christianity. The statue of the Virgin de Candelaria, which is located on Titicaca's southwest shore, dates from 1576 and remains a place of pilgrimage.

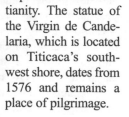

Above: **These boys are poling their balsas, or boats, on Lake Titicaca.**
Right: **Part of an ancient Inca palace on Titicaca Island.**

Of the Earth's tallest mountains, **Mount Everest** (see no. 24) rises the highest above sea level, **Chimborazo** (see no. 17) has its peak most distant from the Earth's center, and **Mauna Kea** (see no. 53) is the tallest from base to peak. The issue of Mauna Kea, which has much of its height below the waters of the **Pacific Ocean**, raises the question: what is the tallest "invisible" mountain on Earth? In other words, what is the tallest seamount whose entire height is contained beneath the sea?

The tallest mountain on Earth that cannot be seen from the surface is the **Tonga Trench Seamount**, which is near the Tonga Trench between Samoa and New Zealand. It was discovered in 1953, the same year that Everest was first climbed by a human.

The Tonga Trench Seamount rises 28,500 feet (8,700 meters) from the ocean floor, but its peak is still 1,200 feet (370 meters) beneath the waves. By contrast, Everest rises about 14,000 feet (4,300 meters) above the **Qinghai-Tibet Plateau**, and Mauna Kea rises 33,480 feet (10,200 meters) above its base on the floor of the Pacific.

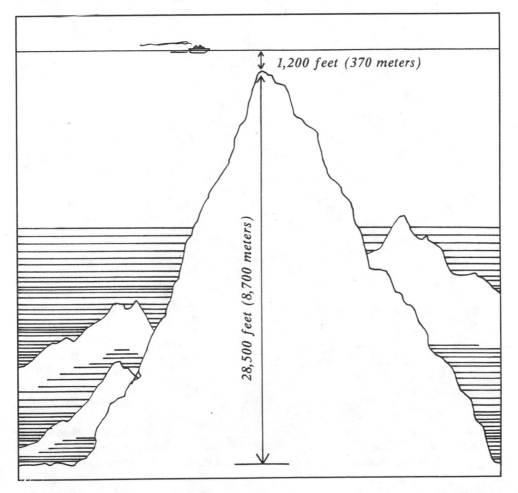

1,200 feet (370 meters)

28,500 feet (8,700 meters)

TRIPLE DIVIDE
Montana, USA

Well over 99 percent of the water carried to the sea by America's rivers and streams drain into either the **Pacific Ocean** or the **Atlantic Ocean** (directly or via the **Gulf of Mexico**). The **Continental Divide**, which runs generally along the crest of the **Rocky Mountains**, separates one drainage route from the other. Yet there is a little-known sliver of land in western Montana where drainage goes into a third ocean — the **Arctic Ocean**.

A second divide, the **Hudson Bay Divide**, intersects the Continental Divide to define another vast land mass that is drained into the Arctic, either directly or via the **Hudson Bay**. Almost all of this land is located within Canada, but a small triangle of about 1,200 square miles (3,100 square kilometers) is found in northwestern Montana. The western part of the triangle is in **Glacier National Park**, and the eastern part, in the **Blackfeet Indian Reservation**.

Contained within this triangle and ultimately draining into the Arctic are the **Upper** and **Lower St. Mary lakes**. The former, with its setting in a semi-circle of alpine peaks, is one of the world's most beautiful lakes, and its image is more often reproduced than any other in the American Rockies.

The point where the Continental Divide intersects the Hudson Bay Divide is at the top of the 8,020-foot (2,440-meter) **Triple Divide Peak**, which is located high among the Montana Rockies, where it overlooks the picturesque alpine lake known to Native Americans as **Medicine Grizzly**. This is the only place in the Western Hemisphere where drainage is into three oceans.

Triple Divide Peak and Pass in Glacier National Park.

While **Bouvet Island** (see no. 13) has the distinction of being the piece of land most remote from any of the Earth's oceans, nobody lives there. The windswept **Tristan da Cunha** has the distinction of being the world's inhabited place that is the farthest from any other inhabited place. Though there are several uninhabited islands nearby, the nearest inhabited land is the island of St. Helena, 1,300 miles (2,100 kilometers) away.

Located in the South Atlantic on a line between Buenos Aires and Cape Town, it was discovered in March 1506 by its namesake, **Tristao da Cunha**, a Portuguese navigator with exploration on his mind. Nobody actually came to the island to live until a hearty soul, named **Thomas Currie**, set foot upon its volcanic shores in 1810. Six years later, it became a British dependency, which it remains today.

The centerpiece of the island is a 6,750-foot (2,060-meter) volcano, whose eruption in 1961 forced the islanders away for two years. Today, about 300 people call Tristan da Cunha "home."

The Tristan da Cunha shoreline.

In the annals of recorded history, it is probable that no volcano has received more mention than Italy's **Mount Vesuvius**, and that no eruption has gotten more attention than the disastrous one that occurred here on August 24 in 79 AD.

Vesuvius is a still-active volcano, the only one of its kind on Europe's mainland. Located nine miles (15 kilometers) southeast of Naples, it stands 4,190 feet (1,280 meters) high. Its crater is presently 709 feet (216 meters) deep and 4,593 feet (1,400 meters) in circumference.

The eruption in 79 AD, which was observed and described by the Roman scholar **Pliny the Younger**, started with an enormous explosion that was followed by a blizzard of ash and sparks. Its final conclusion was a vast tide of lava that buried the cities of Herculaneum, Pompeii and Stabiae and killed an estimated 16,000 people.

Despite subsequent eruptions in 203, 472 and 512, Vesuvius was a tree-covered hill until a massive eruption in 1631 killed 18,000 and swept away the illusion of the volcano's harmlessness. In the twentieth century, explosive and violent eruptions occurred in 1906 (when the whole top blew off), 1929 and 1944.

Two views of Mount Vesuvius erupting in 1906.

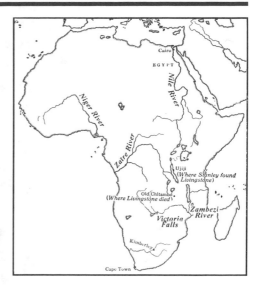

Located on the **Zambezi River** in central Africa on the border between Zambia and Zimbabwe (known as Rhodesia until 1979), the **Victoria (Mosioatunya) Falls** are the world's broadest waterfall. An awesome sight, the falls were so named because the word means "smoke that thunders." Traditionally, the Kololo people of the west avoided them, while the Tonga tribe, who used them in live animal sacrifices, considered them sacred.

The first European to see the falls was the Scottish explorer and missionary David Livingstone, who reached them during his exploration of the Zambezi in 1855 and named them **Victoria Falls** in honor of Queen Victoria.

More than a mile (1.6 kilometers) wide and 400 feet (120 meters) high, the falls carry 30 million tons (27 million metric tons) of water an *hour* during the monsoon season. The falls were formed 500,000 years ago, when the zig-zagging Zambezi zigged across hard basaltic rock and then zagged along a parallel swath of softer sandstone, which began eroding a mile-long trench. Today, the water spilling across the basalt and plunging into the trench is the falls.

Victoria Falls.

Geysers are vertical columns of super-heated water and steam that erupt intermittently when a crack in the Earth's surface goes deep enough to be heated by molten magma in the Earth's interior. Among the world's great geysers, **Old Faithful** in **Yellowstone** (see no. 98) is the most famous and the most regular, but it is not the tallest.

Old Faithful's plume reaches a height of 100 to 180 feet (30 to 55 meters), while the plume of **Steamboat Geyser** in Yellowstone's Porcelain Basin area reaches a zenith of 195 to 380 feet (60 to 115 meters). While Steamboat's eruption is the tallest spewed by any active geyser in the world today, it pales by comparison to New Zealand's mighty **Waimangu**.

Waimangu, whose name is the native Maori word meaning "Black Water," is a violent monster that still lives but has slept for most of the entire twentieth century. The plume of Waimangu was measured at a height in excess of 1,500 feet (460 meters), or 15 times Old Faithful's size. In August 1903, three people were killed during one of its periodic eruptions, which occurred every 30 to 36 hours prior to 1904, when the mighty geyser became inactive. The duration of its inactivity is unknown.

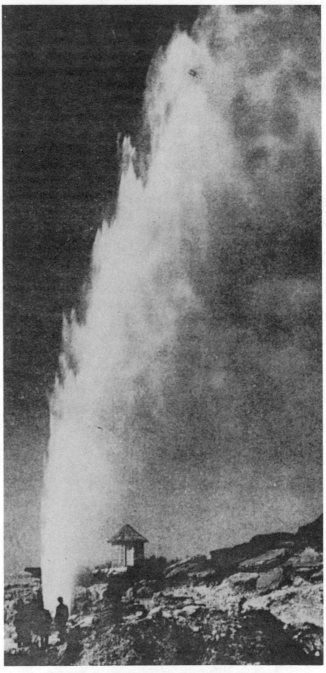

Wairoa Geyser, another of the many geysers in the Rotorua region, circa 1920.

When looking into the water of a lake or sea, we are intrigued by how deep into the water that we can see. Often, because of natural or unnatural material in the water, we cannot see objects that are deeper that two or three times our own height. In mountain lakes, where the water is pure and too cold for high densities of organic material, we can see to the lower depths. This raises the question: Where is the clearest naturally-occurring body of water on Earth?

A great deal has been said about the hardness, softness, purity and clarity of the water that we swim in, sail in and drink. Among waters that are generally uncontaminated by pollutants spilled there by humans, clarity is defined by the water's amount of organic materials (as in swamps) and minerals (as in oceans and in bodies like the **Dead Sea**, the saltiest water on Earth). The clearest water is, therefore, water that has been artificially distilled.

Where then is the clearest naturally-occurring water on Earth, with a clarity approaching that of distilled water? In 1986, Dutch researchers in the **Weddell Sea**, which is off **Antarctica** and 71 degrees south of the equator, discovered that objects lowered into the seawater were visible 262 feet (80 meters) beneath the surface.

An early twentieth century image of the Weddell Seal and the Weddell Sea.

Some of the Earth's most amazing natural wonders are those that cannot be seen. For instance, take the **Tonga Trench Seamount** (see no. 88), which is taller from base to peak than **Mount Everest** (see no. 24), but is entirely under water and invisible from any surface point.

Among the magnificent rivers on Earth, the **Amazon**, which is the biggest and the broadest, carries the greatest volume of water from the land to the sea. At its mouth, the Amazon is 50 miles (80 kilometers) wide. Yet this powerful river is dwarfed by another great river, which is virtually invisible even though it is in plain sight!

The greatest flow of water on Earth is a "river within an ocean," the great **West Wind Drift Current** (or **Antarctic Circumpolar Current**). Located between Antarctica and South America, it flows at a rate of 6.9 billion cubic feet (195 hundred million cubic meters) per second, varying in width from 185 to 1,240 miles (300 to 2,000 kilometers).

The Antarctic Ocean teems with sea birds and marine life.

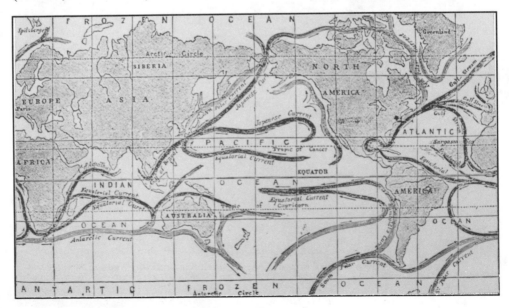

96. YANGTZE RIVER (CHANG JIANG) China

The great **Yangtze** is China's longest river and the world's third-longest after the **Nile** and **Amazon**. It flows for 3,960 miles (6,380 kilometers) on a path that starts at the border of Tibet and China's Qinghai Province, continues through the province of Sichuan (Szechwan) and the great city of Hankow, and finally empties into the East China Sea, which is near Shanghai. (See map on page 44.) The name Yangtze originally applied only to the area at the mouth, as the river itself was traditionally known as **Chang Jiang**, meaning Long River.

As a navigable river, it carries a large volume of traffic. Until the latter part of the twentieth century, the river transported half of China's trade.

A series of gorges on the Yangtze in Sichuan Province are among the most spectacular in the world and rival those of the **Rhine**. Surrounded by steep mountains, they run for 120 miles (190 kilometers) from Fengjie to Yichang and include **Qutang Gorge**, **Wu Gorge** and the river's longest, **Xiling Gorge**.

While the scenery is spectacular — especially the peaks known as the **Twelve Fairy Peaks** in Wu Gorge, created by the Queen of Heaven — the waters are treacherous and unforgiving. The water level can fluctuate radically in flood season, and has been known to rise 170 feet (50 meters).

The gorges have been described with awe and reverence by many observers, including the seventeenth century poet **Du Fu** and the nineteenth century British travel writer **Isabella Bird**, who described their "wild rush . . . spinning down the cataract at tremendous speed into frightful perils."

Above: **The western entrance to Windbox Gorge on the Yangtze River, circa 1935.**

Right: **An early twentieth century view of an old Chinese junk navigating a gorge and rapids on the the Yangtze River.**

In Chinese landscape painting, one occasionally sees images of mountains that are so steep, they seem dramatically exaggerated. One cannot comprehend them as anything but fabrications. But they're not. They really exist.

Located south of the **Yangtze River** and near the border of the Jiangxi and Anhui provinces, there is a mountain range known in the singular as **Yellow Mountain**. It is actually 72 mountains, each unbelievably vertical.

The three tallest, **Guangming Ding** (Summit of Brightness), **Lianhua** (Lotus Flower) and **Tiandu** (Heavenly Capital), are all over 5,900 feet (1,800 meters) high, but their almost straight-up thrust — faithfully recorded by artists through the ages — makes them seem much taller than they actually are.

The ancient writer **Xi Xiake** said that having seen China's five sacred mountains, he couldn't look at ordinary mountains, but after he saw Yellow Mountain, he could no longer look at the five sacred mountains!

The poets have categorized Four Ultimate Beauties embodied by Yellow Mountain: its peaks, its pines, its hot springs that bubble in the valleys between the peaks, and its mists that flow among the peaks, giving them amazing visual depth and making it hard to look at another painting or photograph after you've seen one of Yellow Mountain.

Murmuring Pines in a Mountain Path
Hanging scroll, ink and slight color on silk
painted by T'ang Yin (1470-1523).

In the literature about the great age of human exploration of the planet Earth, which began at the end of the fifteenth century and lasted through the nineteenth century, there are countless stories of explorers beholding natural features that were so spectacular, they defied belief and were so inconceivable, no one back in "civilization" accepted their existence.

Yellowstone Falls.

Such a place that defied belief was that area of northwest Wyoming known traditionally as the **Yellowstone**. Even Native Americans, who'd known about this strange place for generations, found it unbelievable. The first white man to see it was **John Colter**, a member of the 1804-06 Meriwether Lewis-William Clark expedition to the West. His reports of the place, called "Colter's Hell," were written off as hallucinations for almost half a century, but later reports confirmed his stories. In 1871, **Dr. Ferdinand Hayden**, head of the U.S. Geological Survey, led a party into the region to map and photograph its wonders. The area became **Yellowstone National Park**, America's first national park, on March 1, 1872. To this day, with 2.2 million acres (nine hundred thousand hectares) in Wyoming, Montana and Idaho, it is the largest national park in the continental United States.

The centerpiece of the region is the **Yellowstone Caldera**, one of the world's largest and most active calderas. It is a wonderland of boiling hot springs, scalding mud pots and spectacular geysers — including the remarkable **Old Faithful**. These, as well as the awesome **Grand Canyon of Yellowstone**, through which the **Yellowstone River** flows and plunges over **Yellowstone Falls**, owe their existence to the tremendous volcanic forces that have affected the region during the past two million years. Cataclysmic eruptions 2.0, 1.3, and 0.6 million years ago ejected huge volumes of rhyolite magma. Each eruption formed a caldera and extensive layers of thick pyroclastic-flow deposits. The youngest caldera is an elliptical depression that is nearly 50 miles (80 kilometers) long and 30 miles (50 kilometers) wide and occupies much of Yellowstone National Park. The caldera is buried by several extensive rhyolite lava flows that erupted between 75,000 and 150,000 years ago.

The Earth's crust beneath Yellowstone National Park is still restless. Precise surveys have detected an area in the center of the caldera that rose by as much as 34 inches (86 centimeters) between 1923 and 1984 and then subsided slightly between 1985 and 1989. Scientists do not know the cause of these ups and downs, but hypothesize that they are related to the addition or withdrawal of magma beneath the caldera, or to the changing pressure of the hot groundwater system above a vast magma reservoir.

The Yellowstone and the area immediately west of the park are historically among the most seismically active areas in the Rocky Mountains. Small magnitude earthquakes are common beneath the entire caldera, but most occur along the **Hebgen Lake** Fault Zone that extends into the northwest part of the caldera. In 1959, an earthquake measuring 7.5 on the Richter sale happened here.

There are few places on Earth that encompass more scenic beauty for their size than **Yosemite Valley**, which was described by the great naturalist **John Muir** as "the incomparable valley." Here, a wonderland of meadows and cedar forests are both bisected by the surging **Merced River** and surrounded by massive cliffs, which, in turn, are punctuated by massive waterfalls.

Ten miles (16 kilometers) long and less than a mile (two kilometers) wide, Yosemite is the best example of a glacier-carved canyon in the world. Among its most striking geologic features visible from the valley floor are **El Capitan**, a mountain whose sheer granite face rises straight up from the valley to an elevation of 7,569 feet (2,307 meters), and **Half Dome**, an 8,842-foot (2,695-meter) granite dome whose face was ripped away by glaciers millions of years ago. The dome's present appearance is virtually symbolic of Yosemite.

A wonder in itself is Yosemite Falls, in which **Yosemite Creek** travels 2,425 feet (740 meters) from high-above cliffs to the valley below, where it joins the Merced River.

At the urging of men like John Muir, 760,000 acres, including the valley, were set aside as **Yosemite National Park** in 1890.

The classic image of Yosemite Valley from the west.

Just as the nation through which it flows was once known as the Congo, the **Zaïre River** was known until 1971 as the **Congo River**. Its present name means "river," while its former name was for that of the Kongo people, who lived on its lower shores.

Flowing through the heart of Africa for 2,900 miles (4,700 kilometers), the Zaïre River carries the second-largest volume of water of any river on Earth. Located almost directly across the Atlantic Ocean from the Amazon, it is second only to the Amazon in the amount of water that it dumps into the Atlantic Ocean. It rises as the **Lualaba River** near Zambia's border, flows north through a series of waterfalls and whirlpools known as "the Gates of Hell," and finally turns west and south at **Boyoma Falls**, the world's most massive falls in terms of water volume. They were previously known as **Stanley Falls** after **Henry Stanley**, the American explorer who discovered them.

The Zaïre River has long been at the center of legends of mystery and danger. Joseph Conrad summed it up in the title of his novel about the region: *Heart of Darkness*. Among Europeans, the Portuguese explorer Diogo Cao first discovered the river's vast mouth in 1482. It was obviously a major waterway, larger than any in Europe, but a huge waterfall a short distance upstream prevented the Europeans from sailing up it in large boats. The river remained a mystery, spawning the legends of "darkest Africa."

Scottish missionary **David Livingstone** went into the region in the mid-nineteenth century to search for the source of the Congo, which was theorized to be the same as that of the **Nile River**. When Livingstone was thought to have disappeared, the *New York Herald* sent Henry Stanley, then a reporter on the paper, to find him. In 1871, he finally did, calmly walking up to him with the words "Dr. Livingstone, I presume." (See map on page 99.)

The headlines made Stanley a major celebrity, but at the same time, he was immensely enthralled by the difficult, dangerous river, so he returned between 1874 and 1877 to explore the region.

Crocodiles and other denizens of the Zaïre River

TRIVIA QUIZ & GAMES

1. Where on Earth can you find a naturally-occurring group of spindly stone pillars a yard wide at the base and taller than the surrounding trees — and each one has a boulder twice its own diameter balanced on its peak? (See no. 76 Ritten)

2. What is the most remote *inhabited* island in the world? (See no. 90 Tristan da Cunha)

3. Name two monoliths, or gargantuan "single rocks," around whom legends of the supernatural have been associated. (see no. 10 Ayers Rock, and no. 22 Devil's Tower)

4. Where is the place on the Earth's solid surface that is more remote from the world's great seas than any other. (See no. 23 Dzungaria)

5. What is the deepest canyon in the world, measured from the crest of the overlook to the river at the bottom of the gorge? (See no. 44 Kings Canyon)

6. Name a place in the heart of a major American city where the bodies of long-extinct saber-toothed tigers (smilodons) from the Pleistocene epoch lie preserved in asphalt. (See no. 47 La Brea Tar Pits)

7. Where is the wettest place on Earth? (See no. 56 Meghalaya)

8. Sir Arthur Conan Doyle's *The Lost World* is based on the existence of what natural features in what country? (See no. 85 Tepuis)

9. Where is the only place in the western hemisphere where drainage is into three oceans? (See no. 89 Triple Divide)

10. What is the longest mountain range on Earth? (See no. 2 The Andes)

11. What place, originally called "Colter's Hell," was written off as a hallucination for almost half a century? (See no. 98 Yellowstone)

12. What great river frightened many travellers and was immortalized by Joseph Conrad summed in his novel *Heart of Darkness*? (See no. 100 Zaïre River)

13. What is the world's tallest waterfall, twice as high as Yosemite Falls, and 30 times as high as Niagara Falls? (See no. 3 Angel Falls)

14. What place on Earth had no recorded rainfall for the *401 years* between 1570 and 1971? (See no. 7 the Atacama Desert)

15. What are the two tallest mountains in the world and when was the second tallest thought to be the tallest? (See no. 24 Mount Everest)

16. Where is the deepest point on the floor of any of the world's oceans? (See no. 16 Challenger Deep)

17. The summit of what mountain is farther from the center of the Earth than any other? (See no. 17 Chimborazo)

18. What place in the United States is both the hottest and lowest place in the Western Hemisphere? (See no. 21 Death Valley)

19. What is the largest living thing on earth and why was it not discovered until 1992? (See no. 32 The Great Fungus)

20. What is the largest concentration of fresh water on earth? (See no. 33 The Great Lakes)

21. Where is there a naturally-occurring mass of nearly 40,000 six-sided solid stone columns that appear to have been hewn by human hands? (See no. 29 Giant's Causeway)

22. What is the world's highest navigable lake? (See no. 87 Lake Titicaca)

23. Europe's largest lake is so large that Europe's six smallest nations could *all* fit within it as islands. Where is it? (See no. 48 Lake Ladoga)

24. What is the highest mountain on Earth in terms of its height from its base to its peak? (See no. 53 Mauna Kea)

25. What river is renowned in myth and legend as "the Father of Waters?" (See no. 57 Mississippi River)

26. Where on Earth is there a vast river delta with a network of waterways 50 miles (80 km) long and 10 miles (16 km) wide, that leads not into a great body of water, but into oblivion? (See no. 62 Okavango Delta)

27. Where and when was the largest explosion to take place on earth in recorded history? (See no. 80 Santorini)

28. Name the place that Mark Twain called the "loneliest place on Earth," where the waters team with fly larvae, slabs of volcanic rock float in the thick, salty water and the islands are covered with steaming vents of hot springs and with frozen white forests of tufa, spindly spires of calcium carbonate. (See no. 60 Mono Lake)

INDEX

Aegean Sea 87
Africa 11, 20, 40,
   50, 53, 69, 71,
   84, 87, 99
Alaska 62, 73, 79,
   82
Alexander the Great
   22, 47
Alps 59, 81, 83
Amazon River 8, 35,
   74, 102-103, 107
Andes, the 8-9, 14,
   24, 60, 94
Angel Falls 10
Angola 48, 74
Ankarana Plateau
   11
Antarctica 12, 15,
   20, 45, 101-102
Antarctic Circumpo-
   lar Current see
   West Wind Drift
   Current
Antarctic Ice Sheet
   12, 42
Arches National
   Park 13
Argentina 46
Arizona 37
Arctic Ocean 30, 96
Arctic Seals 18, 22
Arctic, the 26
Asia 9, 22, 33, 37,
   75, 93
Atacama Desert 14
Atmosphere, Earth
   15, 80
Atlantic Ocean 8,
   20, 40, 66, 74,
   84, 89, 96, 97,
   102, 107
Augustine, Mount
   79, 82
Aurora Australis and
   Aurora Borealis
   16
Australia 17, 29,
   38, 43, 75

Austria 81, 83
Ayers Rock 17, 29
Babylon 45, 93
Baikal, Lake 18
Baikal Seals 18, 22
Balaton, Lake 19
Bangladesh 35, 63
Black Water Geyser
   see Waimangu
   Geyser
Blue Jets 80
Botswana 48, 74
Bouvet Island 20,
   97
Brahmaputra River
   35, 47
Brazil 8, 46
Brule, Etienne 40,
   91
California 28-29,
   39, 51, 54, 56-
   57, 67-68, 79,
   86, 90, 106
Canada 34, 40, 52,
   70, 91, 96
Carlsbad Caverns
   21
Cascade Range 25,
   56, 78, 85
Caspian Sea 22,
   89, 91
Caves & Caverns
   21, 35, 58, 66,
   72, 88
Challenger Deep
   23, 75
Chang Jiang River
   see Yangtze River
Chicago 40, 63
Chile 14
Chimborazo, Mount
   9, 24, 60, 95
China 9, 30, 44,
   87, 103-104
Churun Meru see
   Angel Falls
Clemens, Samuel
   see Twain, Mark

Congo River see
   Zaïre River
Crater Lake 25
Crocker Land 26
Dead Sea 27, 41,
   100
Death Valley 28
Demoiselles Coif-
   fees see Ritten
Denali see McKinley,
   Mount
Devil's Postpile 29,
   36
Devil's Tower 29
Dzungaria 30
Earthquakes 57, 62,
   79, 82, 85-86
Ecuador 24, 75
Egypt 45, 71, 87
Europe 9, 12, 19,
   53, 55, 75-76,
   81, 87, 98, 107
Everest, Mount 9,
   15, 24, 31, 37,
   60-62, 95, 102
Everglades, the 32
Florida 32, 86
France 81, 83, 87
Fuji, Mount 33
Fuji-san see Fuji,
   Mount
Fundy, Bay of 34
Ganga or Gangaji
   River see Ganges
   River
Ganges River 35
Germany 33, 81
Geysers 100, 105
Giant's Causeway
   29, 36, 42
Glaciers 47, 59, 62,
   78, 106
Gobi Desert 30, 44
Goddess Mother of
   the World see
   Everest, Mount
Gold Rushes 52, 68
Grand Canyon, the

   15, 37-38, 51
Great Barrier Reef
   38
Great Fungus, the
   39, 68
Great Lakes, the 40,
   89, 91
Great Salt Lake 41
Greenland 42, 75
Greenland Ice Sheet
   42
Guam 23, 75
Guiness Book of
   Records 31, 34
Gulf of Mexico 64,
   96
Hawaii 49, 60-61,
   82, 85
Hillier, Lake 43
Himalayan/Karako-
   ram Range 9, 22,
   24, 30-31, 35,
   47, 60
Huang Ho River 44
Huang Shan Moun-
   tain see Yellow
   Mountain
Hungary 19
Huron, Lake 40, 91
Ice Ages 54, 70, 76,
   83
Ice Island of 1956
   and Ice Island T.1
   45
Igazu Falls 46
Illinois 40, 64
India 9, 35, 63, 87
Indian Ocean 30,
   35, 75
Indonesia 53, 82
Indus River 47, 74
Iraq 93
Ireland 29, 66
Israel 27
Italy 31, 83, 98
Japan 33, 75, 79, 82
Jordan 27
Kalahari Desert 48,

74
Kazakhstan 22, 30
Kentucky 58
Kenya 50
Kilauea Volcano 49, 85
Kilimanjaro, Mount 50
Kings Canyon 51
Klondike River 52
Krakatau see Krakatoa
Krakatoa 45, 53, 87
La Brea Tar Pits 54
Ladoga, Lake 55
Lassen Peak 56
Lewis, Meriwether & Clark, William 65, 105
Livingstone, David 99, 107
Long Valley Caldera 57
Los Angeles 82, 86
Luxembourg 75-76
Madagascar 11, 75
Malaysia 77, 88
Mammoth Cave 58
Marinas Trench 23, 75
Mars 12, 15
Matterhorn, the 59
Mauna Kea 15, 49, 60-61, 75, 95
Mauna Loa 49, 61, 75
McKinley, Mount 62
Mediterranean Sea 71, 74
Meghalaya 63
Mesopotamia 25, 87
Mesosphere 15, 80
Mexico 72, 82
Michigan 39-40
Michigan, Lake 40, 91
Minnesota 64, 91
Mississippi-Missouri-Red River System

64-65
Mississippi River 64-65
Missouri 64-65
Missouri River 64-65
Moher, Cliffs of 66
Mono Lake 67
Monoliths 17, 29
Monsoons 63, 99
Montana 65, 96, 105
Monte Cervino see Matterhorn, The
Mosioatunya Falls see Victoria Falls
Mother Lode, the 68
Muir, John 51, 106
Nahr en Nil see Nile River
Namib Desert 69
Namibia 69, 74
Nebraska 57, 65
Nepal 9, 31
Netherlands, The 76, 81
New Guinea 42, 75
New Mexico 21
New York City 70, 88
New York State 40, 70
New Zealand 31, 82, 95, 100
Niagara Falls 10, 46, 70
Nile River 35, 71, 74, 103, 107
Nohoch Na Chich 72
North America 28, 40, 53, 62, 64, 70, 79, 85, 89, 91
North American Plate 82, 86
Northern Ireland 36
Novarupta 73
Okavango Delta 74
Old Faithful 100,

105
Ontario 40, 70, 91
Oregon 25, 90
Pacific Basin 82
Pacific Ocean 8, 9, 23, 34, 45, 60, 74-75, 77, 82, 86, 90, 95-96
Pacific Plate 75, 82, 86
Pakistan 47
Peak XV see Everest, Mount
Peru 8, 94
Pole, North Geographic and South Geographic 12, 16
Polesye see Pripet Marshes
Pripet Marshes 76
Pulau Batu Hairan 77
Qomolangma see Everest, Mount
Quinghai Province 44, 103
Quinghai-Tibet Plateau 60, 95
Rainier, Mount 78
Redoubt, Mount 79
Red Sprites 80
Redwoods see Sequoias
Renon see Ritten
Rhein River see Rhine River
Rhine River 33, 81, 103
Ring of Fire, the 75, 77, 82
Ritten 42, 83
Rocky Mountains 96, 105
Russia 18, 22, 55, 76
Sagarmatha see Everest, Mount
Sahara Desert 48,

71, 84
St. Helens, Mount 56, 73, 82, 85
St. Louis 64-65
San Andreas Fault 79, 86
San Francisco 57, 82, 86
Santorini 45, 53, 68, 87
Sarawak Chambers 88
Sargasso Sea 89
Sequoias, The 90
Shoshones 28, 67
Sierra Nevada Range 51, 57, 67-68, 90
Solimoes River see Amazon River
South America 8-9, 46, 75, 82, 94, 102
South Atlantic see Atlantic Ocean
Southern Hemisphere 12, 16
South Pacific see Pacific Ocean
Stanley, Sir Henry 71, 107
Stratosphere 15, 85
Sumatra 53, 75
Sun, the 16, 34
Superior, Lake 40, 91
Switzerland 59, 81
Tanzania 50
Tepuis, the 92
Thermosphere 15, 80
Tibet 9, 31, 103
Tibetan Plateau 30, 33
Tidal Waves 53, 79
Tigris-Euphrates Valley 93
Titicaca, Lake 9, 94
Tonga Trench

Seamount 95, 102
Toronto 40, 70
Triple Divide 96
Tristan Da Cunha 20, 97
Tsunamis see Tidal Waves
Twain, Mark 64, 67
Uluru see Ayers Rock
United States 13, 15, 21, 25, 28-29, 32, 36-37, 39-41, 49, 51, 54, 56-58, 60-62, 64-65, 67-68, 70, 73, 78-79, 82, 85-86, 90-91, 96, 105-106
US National Forests 51, 67
US National Monuments 13, 21, 28, 37, 56, 73
US National Parks 13, 21, 25, 32, 37, 51, 56, 58, 62, 78, 90-91, 96, 105-106
Utah 13, 41
Venezuela 10, 92
Vesuvius 98
Victoria Falls 46, 99
Victoria, Lake 40
Volcanos 9, 25, 33, 49-50, 53, 56-57, 60-61, 73, 75, 78, 82, 85, 87, 97-98, 105
Waimangu Geyser 100
War of 1812 33, 58
Washington 73, 78, 82, 85
Weddell Sea 101
Western Hemisphere 25, 28, 40, 96
West Wind Drift Current 102
Wisconsin 40, 91
World War II 52, 55
Wyoming 29, 105
Xinjiang Uygur 30
Yangtze River 44, 103-104
Yellow Mountain 104
Yellow River see
Huang Ho River
Yellow Sea 30, 44
Yellowstone 26, 100, 105
Yellowstone River 65, 105
Yosemite Valley 106
Yukon Territory 52
Zaïre 48, 107
Zaïre River 107
Zambia 99, 107
Zimbabwe 48, 99